Journey to the Rooftop of the World: Trekking the Himalayas

Copyright Page

TITLE: Journey to the Rooftop of the World: Trekking the Himalayas

1ST Edition

Copyright @ 2023

ISBN: 9798223038948

Table of Contents

Journey to the Rooftop of the World: Trekking in the Himalayas

By Roberto Miguel Rodriguez

Chapter 1: Introduction to Trekking in the Himalayas

The allure of the Himalayas

Welcome to the majestic Himalayas, a place that will take your breath away and leave you in awe of its natural beauty and spiritual serenity. Journey to the Rooftop of the World: Trekking in the Himalayas invites you to embark on an unforgettable adventure through this enchanting region.

For those seeking an adrenaline rush and a chance to conquer new heights, trekking in the Himalayas offers an unparalleled experience. Immerse yourself in the breathtaking landscapes, from snow-capped peaks to lush valleys, and witness the incredible diversity of flora and fauna that call this region home. Whether you are an experienced trekker or a novice hiker, the Himalayas offer trails suitable for all skill levels, ensuring that there is something for everyone.

Delve into the spiritual heart of the Himalayas by exploring Buddhist monasteries and spiritual retreats. Discover the ancient traditions and teachings of Buddhism, and find solace in the peaceful ambiance of these sacred sites. Allow yourself to be captivated by the mystical chants and ceremonies, and experience a profound sense of tranquility.

Wildlife enthusiasts and birdwatchers will be delighted by the national parks that dot the Himalayan landscape. Get up close and personal with elusive snow leopards, endangered species such as red pandas, and a plethora of bird species that inhabit these protected areas. Capture stunning photographs and create lasting memories as you witness nature's wonders unfold before your eyes.

For the adrenaline junkies, Nepal offers a wide range of adventure sports. Soar through the sky with paragliding, conquer the rapids with white-water rafting, or test your limits with bungee jumping. The Himalayas provide the perfect backdrop for these thrilling activities, ensuring an unforgettable experience.

Escape the chaos of everyday life and rejuvenate your mind, body, and soul with yoga and meditation retreats in the mountains. Immerse yourself in the serene environment, surrounded by towering peaks and pristine nature. Let the ancient teachings and practices guide you towards inner peace and self-discovery.

Discover the rich cultural heritage of Nepal by visiting ancient cities and cultural sites. Explore the architectural marvels, intricate temples, and palaces that tell the stories of a bygone era. Engage with the local communities and learn about their traditional arts and crafts, from thangka painting to wood carving. Immerse yourself in the vibrant tapestry of Nepalese culture.

Indulge your senses with tea plantation tours and organic farming experiences. Learn about the art of tea production, sample aromatic brews, and witness the labor of love that goes into each cup. Immerse yourself in the authentic farming practices and gain a deeper appreciation for sustainable agriculture.

For the adventurous souls, the Himalayas offer the ultimate challenge in mountaineering and climbing expeditions. Push your limits and conquer some of the world's highest peaks, including the legendary Mount Everest. Be rewarded with breathtaking views and a sense of accomplishment that is unparalleled.

Experience the true essence of Nepal through homestays and community-based tourism in rural areas. Immerse yourself in the warm hospitality of local families, learn about their customs and traditions, and contribute to the sustainable development of these communities.

Journey to the Rooftop of the World: Trekking in the Himalayas is your gateway to a world of adventure, spirituality, and cultural immersion. Explore the allure of the Himalayas and create memories that will last a lifetime.

Benefits of trekking in the Himalayas

Trekking in the Himalayas offers an unforgettable experience filled with numerous benefits for adventure enthusiasts, nature lovers, and spiritual seekers. In this subchapter, we will explore the various advantages of embarking on a trekking journey through the majestic Himalayan ranges.

1. Immersion in Nature: The Himalayas, with its awe-inspiring landscapes, scenic valleys, and snow-capped peaks, provide a breathtaking backdrop for trekkers. The beauty of this region, untouched by urbanization, allows tourists to reconnect with nature, breathe in fresh mountain air, and experience the serenity of the surroundings.

2. Physical Fitness: Trekking in the Himalayas is a physically demanding activity that offers an excellent opportunity for fitness and endurance. The challenging terrains, steep ascents, and descents require stamina, strength, and agility, making it an ideal adventure for those seeking to push their physical limits.

3. Spiritual Retreats and Buddhist Monasteries: The Himalayas are home to numerous Buddhist monasteries and spiritual retreats. Trekking in this region allows tourists to immerse themselves in the calm and peaceful ambiance of these sacred places, where they can explore ancient Buddhist teachings, experience meditation practices, and witness the monks' way of life.

4. Wildlife and Birdwatching: Nepal's national parks, located in the Himalayan region, are havens for wildlife enthusiasts. Trekking through these parks gives tourists the opportunity to spot rare and exotic animals like the elusive snow leopard, red panda, and Himalayan musk deer. Additionally, birdwatchers can delight in observing a wide variety of avian species, including the colorful Himalayan Monal and the majestic Lammergeier.

5. Adventure Sports: Apart from trekking, the Himalayas offer a range of thrilling adventure sports. Tourists can indulge in paragliding, rafting in the wild rivers, and bungee jumping from vertigo-inducing heights, providing an adrenaline rush like no other.

6. Yoga and Meditation Retreats: The Himalayas have long been associated with spirituality and inner peace. Many retreat centers nestled in the mountains offer yoga and meditation courses, allowing tourists to rejuvenate their mind, body, and soul in a serene and tranquil environment.

7. Cultural Heritage and Ancient Cities: Nepal possesses a rich cultural heritage and ancient cities that reflect its historical significance. Trekking in the Himalayas provides an opportunity to explore these heritage sites, like Kathmandu's Durbar Square and the ancient city of Bhaktapur, immersing tourists in the rich cultural tapestry of the region.

8. Tea Plantation Tours and Organic Farming Experiences: Trekking routes in the Himalayas often pass through lush tea plantations and organic farms. Tourists can engage in guided tours, learning about tea cultivation and witnessing the traditional methods of organic farming, offering a unique and educational experience.

9. Mountaineering and Climbing Expeditions: For those seeking a greater challenge, the Himalayas are the ultimate destination for mountaineering and climbing expeditions. Trekking serves as a stepping

stone for aspiring mountaineers, allowing them to acclimatize to high altitudes and develop the necessary skills before attempting to conquer the towering peaks.

10. Traditional Arts and Crafts: Nepal is renowned for its traditional arts and crafts, such as thangka painting and wood carving. Trekking routes often pass through villages where tourists can witness these skilled artisans at work and even participate in workshops, gaining insights into the rich artistic heritage of Nepal.

11. Homestays and Community-Based Tourism: Trekking in rural Nepal provides opportunities for tourists to stay in local homestays and engage in community-based tourism. This allows for a more immersive cultural experience, fostering a deeper understanding of the local way of life and supporting sustainable livelihoods for the communities.

In conclusion, trekking in the Himalayas offers a multitude of benefits, including reconnecting with nature, physical fitness, spiritual retreats, wildlife exploration, adventure sports, cultural immersion, and unique experiences. It is an adventure of a lifetime that caters to the interests of a diverse range of tourists and niche enthusiasts.

Planning and preparations for a successful trek

Embarking on a trek in the Himalayas is an exhilarating experience that promises breathtaking views, spiritual enlightenment, and adventurous challenges. However, to ensure a successful and enjoyable journey, proper planning and preparations are essential. Here are some valuable tips for tourists who are considering trekking in the Himalayas.

First and foremost, it is crucial to choose the right trek that suits your fitness level and preferences. The Himalayas offer a wide range of treks, from easy and moderate ones to strenuous and demanding routes. Consider factors such as altitude, duration, and difficulty level before making your decision.

Once you have selected your trek, it is important to start preparing physically. Engage in regular exercise, including cardiovascular workouts, strength training, and hiking to build stamina and endurance. Additionally, consult with a doctor to ensure you are fit for high-altitude trekking and discuss any necessary vaccinations and medications.

Packing the right gear and equipment is another vital aspect of trek preparation. Make sure to bring sturdy and comfortable trekking boots, warm and breathable clothing layers, a waterproof jacket, a hat, gloves, sunglasses, and a backpack. It is also essential to carry a first aid kit, water purification tablets, a sleeping bag, a headlamp, and energy-rich snacks.

Acclimatization is crucial when trekking in high-altitude regions. Allow yourself ample time to adjust to the thin air by incorporating rest days into your itinerary. Hydration is key to preventing altitude sickness, so drink plenty of water and avoid alcohol and caffeine.

Engaging with local guides and porters is highly recommended for a safe and enjoyable trek. These experienced individuals not only assist with navigation but also provide valuable insights into the local culture, flora, and fauna. Moreover, hiring local support helps contribute to the sustainable development of rural communities.

Lastly, respect for the environment, local culture, and traditions is of utmost importance. Leave no trace by carrying out your waste and avoiding damage to natural surroundings. Show reverence when visiting Buddhist monasteries and spiritual retreats, and adhere to their rules and customs. Engage in responsible wildlife and birdwatching practices, and support conservation efforts in national parks.

By meticulously planning and preparing for your trek in the Himalayas, you can ensure a rewarding and unforgettable experience. Immerse yourself in the natural beauty, cultural heritage, and adventure that this majestic region has to offer.

Chapter 2: Trekking Routes in the Himalayas

An overview of popular trekking routes

The Himalayas, with its majestic peaks and breathtaking landscapes, offer a paradise for adventure enthusiasts and nature lovers alike. Trekking in the Himalayas is an experience of a lifetime, allowing you to immerse yourself in the pristine beauty of nature while challenging your physical and mental limits. This subchapter will provide an overview of some of the most popular trekking routes in the region, catering to the diverse interests of tourists seeking different experiences.

For those interested in exploring the spiritual side of the Himalayas, the Annapurna Circuit and Everest Base Camp treks are highly recommended. These routes not only offer stunning views of the mountains but also provide opportunities to visit Buddhist monasteries and partake in spiritual retreats. Immerse yourself in the tranquility of these sacred places and reconnect with your inner self.

If wildlife and birdwatching are your passions, the Langtang Valley trek and the Manaslu Circuit trek are perfect choices. These routes take you through national parks teeming with a wide variety of flora and fauna. Spot rare animals like the red panda and Himalayan tahr, and listen to the sweet melodies of colorful Himalayan birds.

For adrenaline junkies seeking adventure sports, Nepal offers a plethora of options. Experience the thrill of paragliding over the Pokhara valley, raft down the raging rivers of the Himalayas, or take a leap of faith with bungee jumping. These activities are sure to get your heart racing and leave you with unforgettable memories.

For those in search of inner peace and rejuvenation, the mountains of Nepal provide the perfect setting for yoga and meditation retreats. Unwind amidst the serenity of nature and find solace in the silence of the mountains. Let your mind and body find harmony as you practice yoga and meditation in these tranquil surroundings.

Nepal is also a treasure trove of cultural heritage sites and ancient cities. Explore the UNESCO World Heritage Sites of Kathmandu Valley, marvel at the intricate thangka paintings and wood carvings, and witness the rich traditions and customs of the Nepalese people.

If you are interested in experiencing the rural way of life, consider a homestay or community-based tourism in remote villages of Nepal. Immerse yourself in the warmth and hospitality of the locals, learn about organic farming practices, and gain insights into their traditional arts and crafts.

For the adventurous souls looking to conquer the mighty Himalayan peaks, mountaineering and climbing expeditions are available. From the iconic Mount Everest to lesser-known peaks like Island Peak and Mera Peak, challenge yourself and fulfill your dreams of standing atop the world.

In conclusion, the Himalayas offer a wide range of experiences for tourists with diverse interests. Whether you are a nature lover, adventure seeker, spiritual enthusiast, or cultural explorer, there is something for everyone in this majestic region. Embark on a journey to the rooftop of the world and create memories that will last a lifetime.

Everest Base Camp Trek

Embark on the adventure of a lifetime with the Everest Base Camp Trek. This subchapter will be your guide to discovering the breathtaking beauty of the Himalayas and experiencing the thrill of reaching the foot of Mount Everest.

As a tourist looking for an unforgettable trekking experience in the Himalayas, the Everest Base Camp Trek is a must-do. This trek offers a unique opportunity to witness stunning landscapes, encounter diverse flora and fauna, and immerse yourself in the rich culture and traditions of Nepal.

Starting from Lukla, a small town nestled in the mountains, the trek takes you through picturesque Sherpa villages, Buddhist monasteries, and spiritual retreats. Along the way, you will have the chance to interact with the local Sherpa community and gain insight into their way of life.

Nature enthusiasts will be delighted by the wildlife and birdwatching opportunities in the national parks along the trekking route. Spot rare species like the Himalayan monal, snow leopard, and musk deer as you navigate through the lush forests and alpine meadows.

For adventure sports enthusiasts, Nepal offers a range of thrilling activities. After completing the Everest Base Camp Trek, you can indulge in paragliding, rafting, or bungee jumping, taking your adrenaline levels to new heights.

Seekers of peace and tranquility will find solace in the yoga and meditation retreats nestled amidst the majestic Himalayas. Unwind and rejuvenate your mind, body, and soul as you connect with nature and find inner peace.

Nepal is also renowned for its cultural heritage sites and ancient cities. Take a break from trekking and explore the ancient temples, palaces, and squares of Kathmandu, Bhaktapur, and Patan. Immerse yourself in the vibrant culture and witness the exquisite craftsmanship of traditional arts and crafts like thangka painting and wood carving.

For a unique experience, consider staying in a homestay and engaging in community-based tourism in rural Nepal. Learn about organic farming, participate in tea plantation tours, and interact with the warm and welcoming locals.

Lastly, for those with a passion for mountaineering, Nepal offers unparalleled opportunities for climbing expeditions in the Himalayas. Fulfill your dreams of conquering peaks and embark on a mountaineering adventure like no other.

Whether you are seeking adventure, spirituality, cultural immersion, or simply a chance to connect with nature, the Everest Base Camp Trek is the perfect choice. Discover the wonders of the Himalayas and create memories that will last a lifetime.

Annapurna Circuit Trek

Embark on an epic adventure through the heart of the Himalayas with the Annapurna Circuit Trek. This iconic trek is a must-do for any adventurous traveler seeking to explore the stunning landscapes, rich cultural heritage, and spiritual treasures of Nepal.

The Annapurna Circuit Trek is a 128-mile journey that takes you around the Annapurna Massif, offering breathtaking views of towering snow-capped peaks, lush valleys, cascading waterfalls, and quaint mountain villages. As you traverse the diverse terrain, you will witness the dramatic change in scenery, from terraced fields and rhododendron forests to arid high-altitude deserts.

This trek also provides ample opportunities to immerse yourself in the local culture and spirituality. Along the way, you will encounter Buddhist monasteries and spiritual retreats, where you can learn about the ancient teachings and practices of Tibetan Buddhism. Take a moment to meditate amidst the serene surroundings or engage in a conversation with the friendly monks, gaining insights into their way of life.

For wildlife enthusiasts and birdwatchers, the Annapurna Conservation Area offers a sanctuary for a wide variety of species. Keep your eyes peeled for elusive snow leopards, Himalayan tahr, and colorful pheasants as you explore the pristine national parks. The area is also a paradise for adventure sports enthusiasts. Experience the thrill of paragliding over the awe-inspiring landscapes, raft down the roaring rivers, or take a leap of faith with bungee jumping.

Nepal is also renowned for its yoga and meditation retreats, and the mountains provide the perfect backdrop for finding inner peace and serenity. Join a yoga retreat and rejuvenate your mind, body, and soul while surrounded by the majestic Himalayan peaks.

As you make your way through the Annapurna Circuit, you will also encounter ancient cities and cultural heritage sites that reflect Nepal's rich history and artistic traditions. Explore the ancient city of Kathmandu with its intricately carved temples and palaces, or visit the birthplace of Lord Buddha in Lumbini.

For those interested in sustainable tourism, the Annapurna region offers opportunities for homestays and community-based tourism experiences. Spend a few nights with a local family, immersing yourself in their way of life, sharing meals, and learning traditional arts and crafts such as thangka painting and wood carving.

The Annapurna Circuit Trek is also a gateway to mountaineering and climbing expeditions. If you're an experienced climber, challenge yourself to conquer some of the world's highest peaks, including Annapurna I, the tenth highest mountain in the world.

Whether you seek adventure, spirituality, cultural immersion, or a connection with nature, the Annapurna Circuit Trek offers an unforgettable journey through the majestic Himalayas, catering to the diverse interests of every traveler.

Langtang Valley Trek

Langtang Valley Trek: Exploring the Hidden Gem of the Himalayas

Welcome to the subchapter on Langtang Valley Trek, an exhilarating adventure that will take you deep into the heart of the majestic Himalayas. Nestled in the Langtang National Park, this trek offers a unique experience for nature lovers, adventure enthusiasts, and spiritual seekers alike.

The Langtang Valley Trek is a moderate-level trek that can be completed in 7-10 days, making it perfect for those seeking a shorter yet rewarding Himalayan experience. The trek starts from Syabrubesi, a scenic village that serves as the gateway to the Langtang region. As you ascend through lush rhododendron forests, quaint villages, and glacial rivers, the breathtaking views of snow-capped peaks like Langtang Lirung (7,234m) will leave you awe-inspired.

One of the highlights of this trek is the opportunity to visit the ancient Buddhist monasteries nestled in the mountains. These monasteries offer a serene environment for meditation and spiritual retreats, allowing you to immerse yourself in the rich Buddhist culture of the region. The peaceful chants of the monks, the colorful prayer flags fluttering in the wind, and the stunning vistas create a truly transcendent experience.

For wildlife enthusiasts and birdwatchers, the Langtang Valley Trek is a paradise. The Langtang National Park is home to a diverse range of flora and fauna, including rare species like the red panda and the Himalayan tahr. Keep your binoculars handy, as you may also spot elusive birds like the Himalayan monal and the colorful impeyan pheasant.

Adventure sports lovers will find plenty of opportunities to get their adrenaline pumping in Nepal. After completing the Langtang Valley Trek, you can indulge in thrilling activities like paragliding, rafting in the Trishuli River, or bungee jumping from the world's second-highest natural bungee site in Bhote Koshi.

For those seeking inner peace and rejuvenation, the mountains of Nepal offer ideal settings for yoga and meditation retreats. Join a retreat in the tranquil Himalayan villages and let the serene surroundings and expert guidance help you achieve a deeper level of mindfulness and self-discovery.

In addition to its natural wonders, Nepal is also famous for its rich cultural heritage. Extend your stay to explore ancient cities like Kathmandu, Bhaktapur, and Patan, where you can witness stunning architecture, intricate wood carvings, and traditional arts like thangka painting.

If you're a tea lover or interested in organic farming, do not miss the opportunity to visit the tea plantations and organic farms in the region. Learn about the process of cultivating tea leaves and indulge in a cup of freshly brewed tea while soaking in the breathtaking views of the terraced landscapes.

For the adventurous souls, Nepal offers various mountaineering and climbing expeditions in the Himalayas. Test your limits and conquer peaks like Yala Peak or even attempt the ultimate challenge of climbing Everest.

For a truly immersive cultural experience, consider staying in a homestay or participating in community-based tourism in rural Nepal. Engage with the locals, learn about their traditions, and contribute to the sustainable development of these remote communities.

The Langtang Valley Trek is just a glimpse of the wonders Nepal has to offer. Whether you are seeking adventure, spiritual enlightenment, or cultural immersion, Nepal is a destination that will captivate your senses and leave you with memories to last a lifetime. So, pack your bags, lace up your boots, and get ready for an unforgettable journey to the rooftop of the world.

Upper Mustang Trek

The Upper Mustang Trek is a captivating journey through the mystical landscapes of the Himalayas, offering an unforgettable experience for adventure enthusiasts, nature lovers, and cultural explorers. This subchapter will provide you with insights into this unique trek, showcasing its highlights and the incredible experiences it offers.

Located in the remote and restricted region of Mustang, the Upper Mustang Trek takes you to the hidden kingdom of Lo Manthang, an ancient walled city that was once a crucial trading route between Tibet and India. This trek is a blend of natural beauty, cultural immersion, and spiritual enlightenment.

As you venture into the Upper Mustang region, you will be mesmerized by the picturesque landscapes, with barren desert-like terrains contrasted against snow-capped mountains. The trek takes you through deep canyons, eroded cliffs, and unique geological formations, providing a surreal experience that few have witnessed.

One of the highlights of the Upper Mustang Trek is the opportunity to explore ancient Buddhist monasteries and spiritual retreats. The region is home to some of the oldest and most significant monasteries in Nepal, offering a glimpse into the rich Buddhist culture and practices. Immerse yourself in the peaceful ambiance, witness monks chanting their prayers, and discover the profound spiritual teachings that have been passed down for centuries.

For wildlife enthusiasts and birdwatchers, the Upper Mustang region offers a diverse range of species that thrive in the harsh mountain environment. From the elusive snow leopard to the graceful Himalayan blue sheep, this trek provides a chance to spot some of the rarest wildlife in their natural habitat. Additionally, the region is a paradise for birdwatching, with various species of eagles, vultures, and migratory birds soaring through the skies.

Adventure seekers will find delight in the numerous thrilling activities available in Nepal. After completing the Upper Mustang Trek, you can indulge in paragliding, rafting, and even bungee jumping in the breathtaking landscapes of Nepal. Experience an adrenaline rush like never before as you soar through the skies or conquer the raging rivers.

For those seeking peace and tranquility, the mountains of Nepal offer an ideal setting for yoga and meditation retreats. Connect with your inner self amidst the serene surroundings, rejuvenate your mind, body, and soul, and experience the profound benefits of these ancient practices.

The Upper Mustang region is also rich in cultural heritage sites and ancient cities. Explore the UNESCO World Heritage Sites of Kathmandu Valley, visit ancient temples and palaces, and witness the vibrant traditions and customs of the local communities.

Tea plantation tours and organic farming experiences provide an opportunity to learn about sustainable agricultural practices and indulge in the flavors of Nepal's organic produce. Engage with local farmers, pluck tea leaves, and savor the aroma of freshly brewed tea.

For the adventurous souls, Nepal offers mountaineering and climbing expeditions in the Himalayas. Embark on a challenging journey to conquer the towering peaks and fulfill your dreams of reaching the summit.

Immerse yourself in the traditional arts and crafts of Nepal, such as thangka painting and wood carving. Learn from skilled artisans and take home unique souvenirs that reflect the rich cultural heritage of the country.

For a truly authentic experience, opt for homestays and community-based tourism in rural Nepal. Stay with local families, immerse yourself in their daily lives, and contribute to the sustainable development of these communities.

The Upper Mustang Trek is a gateway to discovering the hidden treasures of Nepal. It offers a blend of adventure, spirituality, cultural immersion, and natural beauty that will leave you with memories to cherish for a lifetime.

Chapter 3: Buddhist Monasteries and Spiritual Retreats

Exploring the spiritual side of the Himalayas

The Himalayas, with their majestic peaks and breathtaking landscapes, have long been a destination for adventurers and nature enthusiasts. However, beyond the physical beauty lies a spiritual side that is equally captivating. For those seeking a deeper connection with themselves and the world around them, a journey to the spiritual heart of the Himalayas is an experience like no other.

Buddhist monasteries and spiritual retreats dot the mountainous region, offering a sanctuary for those seeking inner peace and enlightenment. Nestled amidst serene surroundings, these monasteries provide a tranquil space for meditation and reflection. Here, visitors can learn from wise monks, participate in ancient rituals, and gain insights into the teachings of Buddhism. The spiritual energy that permeates these monasteries is palpable and can be transformative for those who open themselves up to it.

The Himalayas are also home to several national parks, where wildlife and birdwatching enthusiasts can connect with nature in a profound way. These protected areas are a haven for a diverse range of flora and fauna, including elusive snow leopards, playful red pandas, and a plethora of bird species. Trekking through these parks offers not only the chance to spot these magnificent creatures but also to immerse oneself in the natural beauty of the Himalayas.

For the adventurous souls, the Himalayas offer a variety of adrenaline-pumping activities. Nepal, in particular, is renowned for its adventure sports such as paragliding, rafting, and bungee jumping. Soaring through the skies, navigating rapids, or taking a leap of faith from towering bridges can be exhilarating experiences that push one's boundaries and ignite a sense of fearlessness.

Yoga and meditation retreats in the mountains provide an opportunity to harmonize the mind, body, and soul. Surrounded by the awe-inspiring beauty of the Himalayas, participants can deepen their practice, learn from experienced yogis, and find serenity in the stillness of the mountains. These retreats offer a chance to disconnect from the distractions of modern life and reconnect with one's inner self.

The cultural heritage sites and ancient cities of Nepal provide a glimpse into the rich history and traditions of the region. Exploring ancient temples, palaces, and UNESCO World Heritage sites allows visitors to immerse themselves in the vibrant culture of Nepal and witness the artistic and architectural marvels of the past.

For those interested in sustainable tourism, tea plantation tours and organic farming experiences provide a chance to learn about traditional agricultural practices and support local communities. These immersive experiences offer a glimpse into the lives of the people who call the Himalayas home and offer a chance to contribute to their sustainable livelihoods.

Mountaineering and climbing expeditions in the Himalayas are a dream come true for adventure seekers. Scaling the towering peaks, braving challenging terrains, and pushing one's physical limits can be a life-changing experience. The Himalayas, with their awe-inspiring vistas and formidable peaks, offer a playground for mountaineers and climbers from around the world.

The traditional arts and crafts of Nepal, such as thangka painting and wood carving, are deeply rooted in the region's culture and history. Visitors can witness the skilled artisans at work, learn about the techniques passed down through generations, and even try their hand at these ancient art forms. The intricate designs and vibrant colors of these crafts reflect the rich cultural heritage of Nepal.

For those seeking an authentic experience, homestays and community-based tourism in rural Nepal provide an opportunity to connect with local communities and learn about their way of life. Staying with a host family, participating in daily activities, and immersing oneself in the local culture can foster a deep appreciation for the resilience and warmth of the people of the Himalayas.

In conclusion, the Himalayas offer a wealth of experiences for tourists seeking a spiritual journey. From Buddhist monasteries and spiritual retreats to adventure sports and cultural heritage sites, the region provides a diverse range of activities that cater to various interests. Whether one seeks inner peace, adrenaline-fueled adventures, or a deeper understanding of the local culture, a visit to the spiritual side of the Himalayas is sure to leave a lasting impression.

Visiting iconic Buddhist monasteries

The Himalayas, with its awe-inspiring landscapes and tranquil environment, have long been a spiritual haven for seekers of inner peace and enlightenment. One of the most significant aspects of this region is its rich Buddhist heritage, which is beautifully preserved in its iconic monasteries. For those who are interested in exploring the spiritual side of the Himalayas, a visit to these monasteries is an absolute must.

The monasteries in the Himalayas are not just places of worship, but also centers of learning and meditation. They exude a sense of tranquility and provide a unique opportunity to connect with one's inner self. The architecture of these monasteries is a testament to the rich cultural heritage of the region, with intricate carvings, vibrant paintings, and prayer wheels adorning their walls.

One of the most famous monasteries in the Himalayas is the Tengboche Monastery in Nepal. Situated at an altitude of 3,867 meters, it offers breathtaking views of Mount Everest and is a popular pit-stop for trekkers on their way to the base camp. The monastery hosts colorful festivals and religious ceremonies, providing visitors with a glimpse into the vibrant Buddhist culture.

Another must-visit monastery is the Hemis Monastery in Ladakh, India. It is the largest and wealthiest monastery in the region and is famous for its annual Hemis Festival, which attracts thousands of tourists from around the world. The monastery houses a vast collection of ancient artifacts, including rare thangka paintings and ancient scriptures.

For a truly immersive experience, tourists can also choose to stay in a monastery as part of a spiritual retreat. This allows them to participate in daily rituals, learn meditation techniques from experienced monks, and gain a deeper understanding of Buddhist philosophy.

Visiting these monasteries not only offers a spiritual experience but also provides an opportunity to support the local communities. Many of these monasteries are involved in community-based tourism initiatives, offering homestays and organic farming experiences. By staying in these monasteries or participating in their activities, tourists can directly contribute to the sustainable development of the region.

In conclusion, a visit to the iconic Buddhist monasteries in the Himalayas is an enriching experience that allows tourists to connect with their spiritual side while immersing themselves in the rich cultural heritage of the region. Whether it is for meditation, learning, or simply marveling at the architectural wonders, these monasteries offer something for everyone on their journey to the rooftop of the world.

Participating in meditation retreats

For those seeking a deeper connection with themselves and the world around them, participating in meditation retreats in the Himalayas can be a life-changing experience. These retreats offer a unique opportunity to disconnect from the chaos of everyday life and immerse oneself in the serene beauty of the mountains, while exploring the ancient practice of meditation.

The Himalayas, with their tranquil atmosphere and breathtaking landscapes, provide the perfect backdrop for introspection and self-discovery. Buddhist monasteries and spiritual retreat centers nestled in these mountains offer various meditation programs tailored to different levels of experience. Whether you are a beginner or an experienced practitioner, you will find a retreat that suits your needs.

During these retreats, participants learn various meditation techniques from experienced teachers who guide them in finding inner peace and clarity. These techniques can range from simple breathing exercises to more advanced practices such as Vipassana or mindfulness meditation. The daily schedule typically includes multiple meditation sessions, supplemented with yoga, mindfulness walks, and discussions on Buddhist philosophy.

Apart from the mental and spiritual benefits, meditation retreats in the Himalayas also provide an opportunity to connect with like-minded individuals from different parts of the world. Sharing experiences and insights with fellow participants can enhance the overall retreat experience and foster a sense of community.

In addition to meditation, these retreats often offer other activities to enrich the experience. Nature walks, visits to nearby monasteries, and cultural exchanges with local communities allow participants to immerse themselves in the rich heritage of the Himalayas. Wildlife and birdwatching enthusiasts can explore the national parks in the region, while adventure enthusiasts can indulge in activities like paragliding, rafting, and bungee jumping.

For those interested in yoga, the Himalayas are a haven for yoga and meditation retreats. Practicing yoga amidst the serene mountains enhances the mind-body connection and offers a unique sense of tranquility. Additionally, visitors can also explore the cultural heritage sites, ancient cities, and traditional arts and crafts of Nepal, providing a well-rounded experience of the country's rich cultural heritage.

Meditation retreats in the Himalayas offer a transformative journey towards self-discovery and inner peace. Whether you are a seasoned meditator or just beginning your spiritual journey, these retreats provide the perfect opportunity to immerse yourself in the serene beauty of the mountains while exploring the depths of your own consciousness. So, pack your bags, leave behind the chaos of daily life, and embark on a soul-stirring adventure in the lap of the Himalayas.

Chapter 4: Wildlife and Birdwatching in National Parks

Discovering the diverse wildlife of the Himalayas

The majestic Himalayan region not only offers breathtaking landscapes and thrilling adventures, but it is also home to an incredible array of wildlife. From rare species to exotic birds, the Himalayas provide an unparalleled opportunity for nature lovers and wildlife enthusiasts to witness some of the most unique creatures on Earth.

The national parks in the Himalayas are a treasure trove of biodiversity. With their dense forests, towering mountains, and meandering rivers, these protected areas provide a safe haven for a wide range of animals. One such park is the Chitwan National Park in Nepal, known for its population of the endangered Bengal tiger and the one-horned rhinoceros. Trekking through the park's trails, tourists can spot various species of deer, wild boars, and even elusive leopards.

For birdwatching enthusiasts, the Himalayas are a paradise. With over 800 species of birds, including the rare Himalayan monal and the colorful Himalayan pheasant, birdwatching in the region is a truly remarkable experience. The Langtang National Park and the Kanchenjunga Conservation Area are particularly renowned for birdwatching, where visitors can spot a myriad of avian species in their natural habitat.

Apart from the national parks, the Himalayas also house numerous Buddhist monasteries and spiritual retreats. These serene and peaceful locations not only provide a chance for spiritual enlightenment but also offer an opportunity to encounter the region's wildlife. From monkeys frolicking near monasteries to the elusive snow leopard found in the higher altitudes, these spiritual retreats provide a unique blend of tranquility and wildlife encounters.

For adventure seekers, the Himalayas offer a wide range of adrenaline-pumping activities. Paragliding over the stunning landscapes, rafting down the fast-flowing rivers, and even bungee jumping from towering suspension bridges are just a few of the thrilling experiences available. These activities not only provide an adrenaline rush but also offer a chance to witness the Himalayan wildlife from a completely different perspective.

As the birthplace of yoga and meditation, the Himalayas are an ideal destination for those seeking inner peace and rejuvenation. Numerous retreats and centers nestled amidst the mountains offer yoga and meditation programs, allowing visitors to connect with their inner selves while surrounded by the awe-inspiring beauty of nature. These retreats often provide opportunities for nature walks and wildlife spotting, creating a harmonious blend of spirituality and wildlife exploration.

The cultural heritage sites and ancient cities of Nepal also offer glimpses into the region's rich history and traditions. From the ancient city of Kathmandu with its intricate temples and palaces to the medieval town of Bhaktapur with its traditional arts and crafts, these sites provide a cultural experience like no other. Visitors can explore traditional arts such as thangka painting and wood carving, immersing themselves in the vibrant local culture.

For those interested in sustainable tourism, homestays and community-based tourism in rural Nepal offer a chance to experience the local way of life while contributing to the well-being of the communities. These immersive experiences allow tourists to witness the close relationship between the locals and their natural surroundings, gaining a deeper understanding of the region's wildlife and conservation efforts.

Finally, for the adventurous souls, mountaineering and climbing expeditions in the Himalayas present the ultimate challenge. Scaling the towering peaks and conquering the world's highest mountains is an experience like no other. These expeditions not only offer a chance to witness the incredible biodiversity of the Himalayas but also provide a sense of accomplishment and awe-inspiring views from the rooftop of the world.

In conclusion, the Himalayas offer a diverse range of wildlife experiences for every type of tourist. Whether it's trekking through national parks, exploring Buddhist monasteries, engaging in adventure sports, or immersing oneself in spiritual retreats, the Himalayas provide an unparalleled opportunity to discover the region's incredible wildlife and natural wonders.

Chitwan National Park

Chitwan National Park: Exploring the Wilderness in Nepal

Welcome to Chitwan National Park, a haven for nature enthusiasts and wildlife lovers alike. Situated in the Terai lowlands of Nepal, this UNESCO World Heritage Site is a treasure trove of diverse flora and fauna, making it a must-visit destination for tourists.

Trekking in the Himalayas may be on your bucket list, but don't miss the opportunity to explore Chitwan National Park. Home to over 700 species of wildlife, including the elusive Bengal tiger and the endangered one-horned rhinoceros, this park offers a unique and thrilling experience. Embark on an unforgettable jungle safari, where you can spot these majestic creatures in their natural habitat. Marvel at the sight of elephants bathing in the Rapti River or witness a playful display of monkeys swinging through the trees.

For those seeking tranquility and spiritual enlightenment, Chitwan National Park is the perfect retreat. Surround yourself with the serene beauty of the lush forests and indulge in meditation and yoga sessions amidst nature's embrace. Immerse yourself in the peaceful ambiance of the park, rejuvenating your mind, body, and soul.

Adventure seekers will find their thrill in Chitwan as well. Engage in thrilling activities like paragliding, rafting, and bungee jumping, all within reach of the park. Feel the rush of adrenaline as you soar through the sky, conquer raging rapids, or take a leap of faith from towering cliffs. Chitwan National Park truly offers an all-encompassing adventure experience.

Beyond the wilderness, immerse yourself in the rich cultural heritage of Nepal. Visit ancient cities like Kathmandu and Bhaktapur, marvel at the intricate wood carvings and vibrant thangka paintings, and witness traditional arts and crafts being meticulously crafted by skilled artisans. Engage in tea plantation tours and organic farming experiences, where you can learn the art of tea-making and sustainable farming practices.

For the ultimate Himalayan experience, embark on mountaineering and climbing expeditions, conquering the towering peaks that have captured the hearts of adventurers for centuries. Whether you're a seasoned climber or a novice seeking a new challenge, the Himalayas offer an array of breathtaking summits to conquer.

Finally, immerse yourself in the warm hospitality of rural Nepal through homestays and community-based tourism. Experience the authentic way of life, learn traditional cooking methods, and participate in local customs and festivities. Engaging with the local communities will undoubtedly leave a lasting impression on your journey.

Chitwan National Park is more than just a wildlife sanctuary; it's a gateway to a world of adventure, spirituality, culture, and natural beauty. So, pack your bags, put on your trekking boots, and get ready to embark on a journey of a lifetime in this breathtaking destination.

Bardia National Park

Bardia National Park: A Wilderness Haven in Nepal

Welcome to Bardia National Park, a hidden gem nestled in the heart of Nepal's lush Terai region. This subchapter will take you on a virtual journey through this incredible national park, offering a glimpse into its stunning landscapes, diverse wildlife, and thrilling adventure opportunities.

Stretching over 968 square kilometers, Bardia National Park is a haven for nature enthusiasts and wildlife lovers alike. As you embark on a trek through its pristine forests, you'll be greeted by a symphony of chirping birds, the rustling of leaves, and the occasional trumpet of an elephant. This park is home to a rich biodiversity, including endangered species like the Bengal tiger, one-horned rhinoceros, and Gangetic dolphin. Keep your binoculars handy as you might spot rare bird species such as the Bengal florican and the Sarus crane.

For adrenaline junkies seeking adventure, Bardia National Park has something for everyone. Discover the thrill of paragliding over the park's vast expanses, with breathtaking views of the Himalayas as your backdrop. Brace yourself for an exhilarating white-water rafting experience, navigating the rapids of the Karnali River. And if you're feeling daring, why not try bungee jumping from one of Nepal's highest suspension bridges?

For those seeking inner peace and spiritual rejuvenation, Bardia offers a tranquil setting for yoga and meditation retreats. Immerse yourself in the serene ambiance of the park, surrounded by towering trees and the gentle flow of the Karnali River. Unwind, reflect, and find solace in this natural sanctuary.

As you explore the park, don't miss the opportunity to delve into Nepal's rich cultural heritage. Visit ancient cities and witness the intricate art of thangka painting and wood carving, both integral parts of Nepal's traditional arts and crafts. Engage in homestays and community-based tourism experiences, immersing yourself in the local way of life and fostering connections with the warm and welcoming Nepali people.

Bardia National Park also offers unique tea plantation tours and organic farming experiences, providing a glimpse into sustainable agricultural practices and the opportunity to sample Nepal's famous tea.

Whether you're a wildlife enthusiast, an adventure seeker, a spiritual seeker, or a cultural explorer, Bardia National Park promises an unforgettable experience. So, lace up your boots, pack your sense of adventure, and get ready to embark on a journey through this pristine wilderness.

Koshi Tappu Wildlife Reserve

Koshi Tappu Wildlife Reserve: Exploring Nepal's Biodiversity Haven

Nestled in the eastern Terai region of Nepal, the Koshi Tappu Wildlife Reserve is a hidden gem for nature enthusiasts seeking an unforgettable adventure. Spread over an area of 175 square kilometers, this protected area offers a unique blend of wildlife, wetlands, and cultural heritage that will leave you in awe.

For wildlife enthusiasts, Koshi Tappu is a paradise. Home to over 500 species of birds, including endangered species like the Bengal Florican and Sarus Crane, this reserve is a dream come true for birdwatchers. Embark on a thrilling birdwatching excursion and witness an enchanting symphony of colors and melodies of these feathered creatures. The reserve is also home to numerous mammal species, such as the Gangetic Dolphin, wild water buffalo, and the elusive Bengal tiger. Prepare to be captivated by the sight of these majestic creatures roaming freely in their natural habitat.

Beyond the wildlife, Koshi Tappu offers a plethora of activities for adventure enthusiasts. Brace yourself for an adrenaline-pumping rafting expedition along the serene Koshi River, where you can conquer exhilarating rapids while taking in breathtaking views of the surrounding landscapes. If you're feeling daring, indulge in the thrill of bungee jumping from the nearby suspension bridge, as you embrace the rush of free-falling amidst the stunning backdrop of the Himalayas.

For those seeking a spiritual retreat, Koshi Tappu is the perfect destination to rejuvenate your mind, body, and soul. Immerse yourself in the tranquil ambiance of Buddhist monasteries, where you can meditate and find solace amidst the serene surroundings. Join a yoga retreat and practice ancient techniques amidst the peaceful mountains, allowing yourself to connect with nature and find inner peace.

If you're a culture aficionado, Koshi Tappu will take you on a journey through Nepal's rich heritage. Visit ancient cities like Bhaktapur and Patan, where you can witness the intricate craftsmanship of traditional arts and crafts, such as thangka painting and wood carving. Experience the warmth of Nepali hospitality through homestays and community-based tourism in rural areas, where you can immerse yourself in local traditions and customs.

To top it all off, embark on a tea plantation tour and organic farming experience, where you can learn about Nepal's agriculture practices and indulge in the flavors of freshly brewed tea. And for the adventurous souls, Koshi Tappu serves as a gateway to the majestic Himalayas, offering mountaineering and climbing expeditions for those seeking the ultimate adrenaline rush.

Whether you're a wildlife enthusiast, an adventure seeker, a spiritual seeker, or a culture lover, Koshi Tappu Wildlife Reserve has something to offer for everyone. So, pack your bags, put on your trekking shoes, and get ready for an unforgettable journey to the rooftop of the world.

Chapter 5: Adventure Sports in Nepal

Paragliding over the Himalayas

Have you ever dreamed of soaring through the sky like a bird, with the majestic peaks of the Himalayas beneath you? Look no further than the thrilling adventure of paragliding over the Himalayas. This exhilarating experience offers tourists a unique perspective of the world's highest mountain range and an unmatched adrenaline rush.

Paragliding in Nepal has gained popularity among adventure enthusiasts from around the world. With its diverse landscapes and challenging terrains, Nepal offers the perfect conditions for paragliding. The stunning valleys, lush green forests, and snow-capped peaks of the Himalayas create a breathtaking backdrop for this once-in-a-lifetime experience.

As you prepare to take flight, you'll be equipped with state-of-the-art paragliding gear and receive thorough instructions from experienced pilots. Once you're ready, you'll launch into the air, feeling the wind beneath your wings and the thrill of freedom. As you soar above the Himalayas, you'll witness the awe-inspiring beauty of the mountains, valleys, and rivers that make this region so enchanting.

The paragliding routes in Nepal cater to all levels of experience, from beginners to advanced flyers. Whether you're a first-time paraglider or a seasoned pro, there's a route that will suit your skills and preferences. Some popular paragliding spots include Pokhara, Sarangkot, and Bandipur, each offering its own unique panoramic views of the Himalayas.

Paragliding in Nepal is not just about the adrenaline rush; it's also an opportunity to connect with nature and experience the spiritual energy of the Himalayas. As you glide through the air, you'll be captivated by the serene beauty of the surroundings, feeling a sense of peace and tranquility enveloping you. It's a chance to escape the chaos of everyday life and truly immerse yourself in the serenity of the mountains.

For those seeking a spiritual journey, paragliding over the Himalayas can be combined with visits to Buddhist monasteries and spiritual retreats. Nepal is known for its rich Buddhist heritage, and exploring these ancient sites can provide a deeper understanding of the region's cultural and spiritual significance.

So, if you're an adventure seeker, nature lover, or simply looking for a unique experience, paragliding over the Himalayas is an absolute must. Whether you're gliding above the snow-capped peaks, floating amidst the clouds, or descending into lush valleys, this thrilling adventure will leave you with memories that will last a lifetime. Don't miss out on the opportunity to witness the breathtaking beauty of the Himalayas from above – it's an experience like no other.

Rafting in the raging rivers

If you are an adventure seeker looking for an adrenaline-pumping experience, then rafting in the raging rivers of the Himalayas is an absolute must-do activity. Nepal, situated in the lap of the majestic Himalayas, offers some of the most thrilling and challenging white-water rafting experiences in the world.

With its numerous rivers flowing down from the snow-capped peaks, Nepal is a paradise for both beginners and experienced rafters. The country boasts a wide range of rivers, each offering a unique rafting experience. From the wild and untamed rapids of the Bhote Koshi and Trishuli rivers to the remote and pristine Karnali and Tamur rivers, there is something for everyone.

Rafting in Nepal not only provides an exhilarating experience but also gives you a chance to immerse yourself in the breathtaking natural beauty of the Himalayan landscapes. As you navigate through the gushing waters, surrounded by lush green forests, towering mountains, and cascading waterfalls, you will feel a sense of awe and wonder.

Moreover, rafting in Nepal is not just about the thrill and adventure; it is also an opportunity to connect with the local culture and traditions. Along the way, you will pass through quaint riverside villages, where you can witness the daily lives of the local communities. You might even have a chance to interact with them, learn about their customs, and taste authentic Nepali cuisine.

Safety is of utmost importance when it comes to rafting, and Nepal has a number of professional rafting operators who prioritize your well-being. These operators provide trained guides, top-quality equipment, and adhere to international safety standards, ensuring a safe and enjoyable experience for all.

Whether you are a solo traveler, a group of friends, or a family looking for a thrilling adventure, rafting in the raging rivers of Nepal is an experience you will never forget. So, pack your bags, put on your life jacket, and get ready to plunge into the wild and untamed waters of the Himalayas. It's time to make memories that will last a lifetime!

Bungee jumping in the thrilling canyons

As you embark on your journey to the rooftop of the world, the Himalayas, prepare yourself for an adrenaline-pumping adventure that will take you to the very edge of excitement. In this subchapter, we invite you to experience the heart-pounding thrill of bungee jumping in the mesmerizing canyons of Nepal.

Nestled amidst the majestic mountains, Nepal offers a unique opportunity for adventure enthusiasts to take a leap of faith and embrace the sheer exhilaration of bungee jumping. With its towering cliffs and deep gorges, the canyons of Nepal provide the perfect backdrop for this daring activity, promising an experience that will leave you breathless.

Imagine standing on a platform, ready to take the plunge, as the rushing river below beckons you. Feel the cool mountain breeze on your face as you prepare to defy gravity and soar through the air. As you leap into the void, a surge of adrenaline courses through your veins, making you truly feel alive. The feeling of weightlessness is unlike anything you've ever experienced, as you are suspended mid-air, surrounded by the breathtaking beauty of the Himalayan landscape.

The thrill of bungee jumping in Nepal extends beyond the physical sensation. It offers a unique opportunity to connect with the spiritual energy that permeates this land. Nepal is renowned for its Buddhist monasteries and spiritual retreats, where seekers of inner peace and enlightenment find solace. The act of bungee jumping can serve as a metaphor for letting go of fears and inhibitions, allowing you to embrace the present moment and tap into your inner strength.

For wildlife enthusiasts and birdwatchers, bungee jumping in Nepal brings an added bonus. The canyons are home to a diverse array of flora and fauna, offering glimpses of rare and endangered species. As you soar through the air, keep your eyes peeled for the sight of soaring eagles, playful monkeys, and maybe even the elusive snow leopard.

So, dear adventure-seeker, if you're ready to push your boundaries and embark on an unforgettable journey, bungee jumping in the thrilling canyons of Nepal awaits you. Indulge in the heart-stopping excitement that only the Himalayas can offer, and let this experience become a cherished memory of your time in this enchanting land.

Chapter 6: Yoga and Meditation Retreats in the Mountains

Embracing tranquility through yoga

In the hustle and bustle of our modern lives, finding moments of tranquility can be a challenge. However, nestled amidst the majestic Himalayas, there is a place where serenity and inner peace can be discovered through the practice of yoga. Welcome to the subchapter, "Embracing Tranquility Through Yoga," where we explore the transformative power of this ancient practice in the enchanting setting of Nepal.

For those embarking on a trekking adventure in the Himalayas, yoga offers a perfect complement to the physical challenges of the journey. As you traverse through breathtaking landscapes and immerse yourself in the beauty of nature, yoga provides a way to connect with your surroundings on a deeper level. Whether it's a gentle stretch at the start of the day or a peaceful meditation at sunset, yoga can help you find balance and clarity amidst the rugged terrain.

But Nepal is not just about trekking. It is also a haven for seekers of spiritual enlightenment. With its rich Buddhist heritage, the country boasts numerous monasteries and spiritual retreats where visitors can delve into the teachings of Buddhism and experience the tranquility that comes from a deep spiritual practice. Immerse yourself in the soothing chants of monks, explore the ancient rituals, and let the wisdom of the Himalayas guide you on your spiritual journey.

For those interested in wildlife and birdwatching, Nepal's national parks offer a unique opportunity to witness the beauty of nature up-close. And what better way to connect with nature than through the practice of yoga? Imagine performing your sun salutations amidst a chorus of chirping birds or finding inner peace as you observe the graceful movements of wildlife. Yoga and nature intertwine seamlessly, allowing you to find tranquility not only within yourself but also in the natural world around you.

While Nepal is a land of inner reflection, it is also a place for adventure and adrenaline. From paragliding and rafting to bungee jumping, Nepal offers a wide range of thrilling activities. And after an exhilarating day, what better way to wind down than with a yoga and meditation retreat in the mountains? Rejuvenate your body and mind, and let the stunning backdrop of the Himalayas inspire your practice.

Nepal is a treasure trove of cultural heritage, ancient cities, and traditional arts and crafts. Immerse yourself in the vibrant culture, visit UNESCO World Heritage Sites, and explore the intricate thangka paintings and wood carvings that have been passed down through generations. And amidst all this, don't forget to take a moment to embrace tranquility through yoga - a practice that has been an integral part of Nepal's cultural fabric for centuries.

Whether you're seeking adventure, spiritual awakening, or simply a break from the chaos of everyday life, Nepal has something to offer everyone. From yoga and meditation retreats to trekking in the Himalayas, this enchanting country invites you to embrace tranquility and embark on a transformative journey of self-discovery. So, come and experience the magic of Nepal, where the rooftop of the world awaits you with open arms.

Meditation practices amidst breathtaking scenery

The Himalayas, with its awe-inspiring landscapes and serene atmosphere, offers the perfect setting for practicing meditation. In this subchapter, we delve into the various meditation practices that can be undertaken amidst the breathtaking scenery of the Himalayas.

For those seeking inner peace and spirituality, the Buddhist monasteries and spiritual retreats nestled within the mountains provide an ideal environment for meditation. These ancient centers of wisdom offer guidance on different meditation techniques, including mindfulness, loving-kindness, and Vipassana. Immerse yourself in the tranquility of these monastic retreats and experience the true essence of meditation.

The Himalayas are also home to a rich variety of wildlife and bird species, making it a paradise for nature enthusiasts. Engaging in meditation amidst the harmonious sounds of chirping birds and the gentle rustling of leaves can truly elevate the experience. National parks such as Chitwan and Bardia offer designated meditation spots where you can connect with nature and find solace in its beauty.

For adventure seekers, combining meditation with exciting activities is a unique way to experience the Himalayas. Imagine practicing meditation while paragliding over the majestic mountains or finding inner calm amidst the rush of white-water rafting. Bungee jumping enthusiasts can even incorporate meditation techniques to find focus and conquer their fears.

Yoga and meditation retreats are increasingly popular in the Himalayas, attracting individuals who seek holistic wellness and rejuvenation. These retreats offer a blend of yoga, meditation, and pranayama (breathing exercises) amidst the breathtaking mountain scenery. Unwind, recharge, and find your inner balance amidst the serenity of the Himalayas.

Nepal's cultural heritage sites and ancient cities provide a unique backdrop for meditation. The ancient temples and historical landmarks exude a sense of spiritual energy, making them ideal places for quiet contemplation. Engaging in meditation surrounded by centuries-old architecture and sacred sites allows for a deep connection with Nepal's rich cultural heritage.

Tea plantation tours and organic farming experiences provide an opportunity to combine meditation with sustainable practices. Engage in mindful farming or sip a cup of freshly brewed tea while meditating amidst the lush greenery of the Himalayan tea gardens. Connect with the earth and find harmony within yourself and the environment.

For the adventurous souls, meditation can be integrated into mountaineering and climbing expeditions. The solitude and vastness of the Himalayas offer a unique space for self-reflection and introspection. Meditate at base camps or high-altitude camps, and experience the transformative power of the mountains.

Exploring traditional arts and crafts like thangka painting and wood carving can also be a meditative experience. Engage in these ancient art forms, where focus and concentration are paramount. Feel the serenity of the mountains envelop you as you immerse yourself in the creative process.

Lastly, for a more immersive experience, consider staying with local communities through homestays and community-based tourism. Engage in their daily activities and witness their way of life. Meditate amidst the simplicity of rural Nepal and embrace the warmth and hospitality of the locals.

The Himalayas offer a myriad of opportunities for meditation amidst breathtaking scenery. Whether you seek adventure, spirituality, or simply a moment of tranquility, the mountains are calling. Embark on a journey of self-discovery and find your inner peace amidst the Himalayan paradise.

Retreat centers for rejuvenation and self-discovery

In the midst of the majestic Himalayas lies a haven for those seeking solace, inner peace, and personal transformation. Nepal is not only renowned for its breathtaking landscapes and thrilling adventures, but it also offers a plethora of retreat centers that cater to the needs of tourists looking for rejuvenation and self-discovery.

Immerse yourself in the spiritual realm of Buddhism by visiting the numerous monasteries and spiritual retreats nestled in the Himalayan foothills. These serene and secluded spaces provide the perfect environment for meditation, contemplation, and self-reflection. Engage in mindfulness practices, attend Buddhist teachings, and enjoy the calming presence of the resident monks.

For nature enthusiasts, Nepal's national parks offer a unique opportunity to connect with wildlife and indulge in birdwatching. Experience the thrill of spotting rare and exotic species in their natural habitat. These parks also serve as a peaceful backdrop for meditation and yoga sessions, allowing you to find your center amidst the beauty of nature.

Adventure seekers can find their adrenaline fix in Nepal's renowned adventure sports. Whether it's paragliding over the stunning landscapes, rafting through the raging rivers, or bungee jumping from towering heights, these activities provide an exhilarating escape from the mundane and an opportunity to challenge oneself.

Escape the chaos of daily life and delve into the ancient practices of yoga and meditation in the tranquil mountains of Nepal. Retreat centers offer various programs and workshops, led by experienced instructors, to help you unwind, find inner balance, and nourish your mind, body, and soul.

Nepal's rich cultural heritage and ancient cities offer a fascinating glimpse into the country's history and traditions. Explore the UNESCO World Heritage Sites, wander through ancient temples and palaces, and immerse yourself in the vibrant local culture and traditions.

For those interested in sustainable tourism, Nepal's tea plantations and organic farming experiences provide an opportunity to learn about traditional farming practices and indulge in the flavors of fresh, organic produce. Engage in hands-on activities and gain insight into the importance of sustainable agriculture.

Embark on a mountaineering or climbing expedition in the Himalayas and challenge yourself to reach new heights. Whether you're a seasoned climber or a novice adventurer, Nepal offers a range of expeditions to suit all levels of experience.

Discover the intricate art forms of Nepal through workshops on thangka painting and wood carving. Learn from skilled artisans and create your own masterpiece, immersing yourself in the rich cultural heritage of the country.

Experience the warmth and hospitality of rural Nepal through homestays and community-based tourism. Engage with local communities, participate in their daily activities, and gain a deeper understanding of their way of life.

Nepal's retreat centers provide the perfect escape for rejuvenation and self-discovery. Whether you seek spiritual enlightenment, adventure, cultural immersion, or simply a break from the chaos of everyday life, Nepal offers an array of experiences to cater to your interests and needs. Uncover the secrets of the Himalayas and embark on a transformative journey unlike any other.

Chapter 7: Cultural Heritage Sites and Ancient Cities of Nepal

Exploring the rich history and architecture of Nepal

Nestled in the lap of the majestic Himalayas, Nepal is a country steeped in rich history and awe-inspiring architecture. From ancient temples to medieval palaces, this land of enchantment offers an unforgettable journey through time. In this subchapter, we delve into the fascinating history and architectural wonders that await you in Nepal.

Dating back to the 3rd century BC, Nepal has been a cultural crossroads for centuries. Its strategic location on the ancient trade routes between India and Tibet has shaped the country's unique blend of Hindu and Buddhist traditions. As you trek through the Himalayas, you will encounter numerous Buddhist monasteries and spiritual retreats, where you can immerse yourself in the serene ambiance and witness the devotion of the monks.

Nepal is also home to an abundance of wildlife and national parks, making it a paradise for wildlife enthusiasts and birdwatchers. Explore the dense forests of Chitwan National Park and Bardia National Park, where you can spot rare species such as the Bengal tiger, one-horned rhinoceros, and many exotic birds.

For adrenaline junkies seeking adventure, Nepal offers a wide range of thrilling activities. Experience the rush of paragliding over the picturesque Pokhara Valley, raft down the raging rivers of Trishuli and Bhote Koshi, or take a leap of faith with bungee jumping from the world's highest suspension bridge.

Immerse yourself in the serenity of the Himalayas with yoga and meditation retreats, where you can rejuvenate your mind, body, and soul amidst breathtaking mountain vistas. Nepal's mountainous terrain is also dotted with ancient cultural heritage sites and cities, such as Kathmandu, Bhaktapur, and Patan, where you can explore intricately carved temples, palaces, and lively marketplaces.

Experience the tranquility of rural life with homestays and community-based tourism, where you can interact with the warm and welcoming locals. Engage in tea plantation tours and organic farming experiences, discovering the sustainable practices that have been passed down through generations.

For the adventurous souls, Nepal offers unparalleled opportunities for mountaineering and climbing expeditions in the Himalayas. Summit the iconic peaks of Everest, Annapurna, or Langtang, and experience the triumph of conquering nature's giants.

No journey to Nepal is complete without delving into its rich artistic heritage. Discover traditional arts and crafts, such as thangka painting and wood carving, and witness the skill and precision that goes into creating these intricate masterpieces.

From the ethereal beauty of its landscapes to the vibrant tapestry of its culture, Nepal promises an unforgettable adventure that will leave you with a lifetime of memories. Embark on a journey to this rooftop of the world, and let Nepal's rich history and architecture captivate your senses.

Kathmandu Durbar Square

Kathmandu Durbar Square: Exploring Nepal's Cultural Heritage

Welcome to Kathmandu Durbar Square, a UNESCO World Heritage Site and one of the most captivating attractions in Nepal. This ancient city square is located in the heart of Kathmandu, the capital of Nepal, and is a must-visit destination for tourists who are interested in exploring the rich cultural heritage of the country.

Kathmandu Durbar Square is a historical site that dates back to the 12th century when the Malla dynasty ruled over the Kathmandu Valley. The square is home to several palaces, temples, and courtyards that showcase the architectural brilliance of the Newar people, the indigenous inhabitants of the valley.

As you wander through the square, you will be mesmerized by the intricately carved wooden windows, doorways, and balconies of the ancient palaces. The Hanuman Dhoka Palace, the former royal residence, is a prime example of the Newar architecture and is a significant attraction within the square.

The square is also home to numerous temples, each with its own unique design and religious significance. The Taleju Temple, the oldest temple in the square, is dedicated to the Hindu goddess Taleju Bhawani and is a sacred site for both Hindus and Buddhists. The Kumari Ghar, or the House of the Living Goddess, is another notable temple where you can catch a glimpse of the Kumari, a young girl revered as the living embodiment of the Hindu goddess Taleju.

Apart from the palaces and temples, Kathmandu Durbar Square is also a hub for traditional arts and crafts. You can explore the narrow alleys surrounding the square to find shops selling exquisite thangka paintings, wood carvings, and other handicrafts made by local artisans. This is a perfect opportunity to take home a piece of Nepal's rich artistic heritage.

For those seeking spiritual retreats, Kathmandu Durbar Square offers a serene environment for meditation and self-reflection. You can find quiet corners within the square or visit nearby Buddhist monasteries to immerse yourself in the peaceful ambiance and learn from experienced monks.

Kathmandu Durbar Square is not just a cultural haven, but it is also a gateway to other adventures in Nepal. From here, you can embark on trekking expeditions to the Himalayas, explore national parks for wildlife and birdwatching, indulge in adventure sports like paragliding and rafting, or join yoga and meditation retreats in the mountains.

If you are interested in immersing yourself in the local way of life, you can opt for homestays and community-based tourism in rural Nepal, where you can experience organic farming and participate in traditional activities.

In conclusion, Kathmandu Durbar Square is a captivating destination for tourists interested in exploring Nepal's cultural heritage. Whether you are drawn to ancient cities, religious sites, traditional arts and crafts, or adventure sports, this historical square has something for everyone. So, come and embark on a journey to Kathmandu Durbar Square and immerse yourself in the rich tapestry of Nepal's cultural and natural beauty.

Bhaktapur Durbar Square

Bhaktapur Durbar Square: A Hidden Treasure of Nepal

Welcome to Bhaktapur Durbar Square, a hidden treasure nestled in the heart of Nepal. This enchanting subchapter of our book, "Journey to the Rooftop of the World: Trekking in the Himalayas," is dedicated to all the intrepid tourists seeking a unique and immersive experience in Nepal.

Bhaktapur Durbar Square is a UNESCO World Heritage Site and one of the three ancient royal cities of the Kathmandu Valley. Steeped in history and culture, this square takes you back in time with its exquisite architecture, intricate wood carvings, and awe-inspiring temples. As you wander through its narrow alleyways, you'll be transported to a bygone era, where time seems to stand still.

For the avid trekkers and nature enthusiasts among you, Bhaktapur serves as the perfect base camp for your Himalayan adventures. From here, you can embark on breathtaking treks that offer stunning views of the majestic Himalayan peaks, including Everest, Annapurna, and Langtang. Immerse yourself in the serenity of Buddhist monasteries and spiritual retreats along the way, finding solace in their tranquil surroundings.

If wildlife and birdwatching are your passions, Nepal's national parks will not disappoint. Just a short distance from Bhaktapur, you can explore Chitwan and Bardia National Parks, home to a diverse range of flora and fauna, including the endangered Bengal tiger and the one-horned rhinoceros. Capture unforgettable moments as you witness these majestic creatures in their natural habitat.

For the adrenaline junkies seeking adventure sports, Nepal offers a plethora of options. Experience the thrill of paragliding, rafting down the raging rivers, or bungee jumping off towering cliffs. Nepal is a playground for adventure seekers, and Bhaktapur provides a serene sanctuary to unwind after an adrenaline-filled day.

If you're yearning for inner peace and self-discovery, Nepal is renowned for its yoga and meditation retreats. Nestled amidst the mountains, these retreats offer a perfect blend of spirituality and tranquility, allowing you to reconnect with yourself and find solace in nature's embrace.

Cultural enthusiasts will be enthralled by Bhaktapur's rich heritage. Explore the ancient cities of Nepal, with their elaborate palaces, temples, and courtyards. Witness traditional arts and crafts, such as thangka painting and wood carving, as skilled artisans bring their masterpieces to life.

For a unique experience, immerse yourself in the local culture through homestays and community-based tourism in rural Nepal. Engage with the warm-hearted locals, learn about their customs, and savor traditional cuisine prepared with love and care.

Last but not least, embark on mountaineering and climbing expeditions in the Himalayas, testing your limits and conquering the world's highest peaks. Nepal's mountains offer a challenge like no other, and Bhaktapur serves as a gateway to these awe-inspiring adventures.

So, whether you're seeking spiritual enlightenment, adrenaline-fueled experiences, or a cultural immersion, Bhaktapur Durbar Square is a must-visit destination on your journey to the rooftop of the world. Come, explore, and discover the magic of Nepal.

Patan Durbar Square

Welcome to the enchanting world of Patan Durbar Square! This subchapter will take you on a journey through the mesmerizing historic heart of Patan, an ancient city located in the Kathmandu Valley of Nepal. Steeped in rich cultural heritage and adorned with intricate architectural wonders, Patan Durbar Square is a must-visit destination for any traveler seeking to immerse themselves in the magic of Nepal.

As you step into Patan Durbar Square, you will be greeted by an awe-inspiring array of palaces, temples, and courtyards, each telling a unique story of the city's glorious past. The square is a UNESCO World Heritage Site and is renowned for its exquisite Newari craftsmanship that is evident in every nook and cranny. Marvel at the stunning architecture of the Krishna Mandir, a temple dedicated to Lord Krishna, or lose yourself in the intricately carved wooden windows and doors of the Patan Museum.

For the adventure enthusiasts among you, Patan Durbar Square offers a gateway to a plethora of thrilling activities. From paragliding through the breathtaking Himalayan landscapes to bungee jumping off the towering bridges, this city has it all. You can also indulge in white-water rafting in the gushing rivers or embark on a wildlife safari in one of Nepal's national parks, where you can spot rare and exotic species of birds and animals.

If you seek solace and inner peace, Patan Durbar Square is a spiritual haven. The city is dotted with Buddhist monasteries and spiritual retreats, where you can engage in meditation and yoga practices to rejuvenate your mind, body, and soul. The mountains surrounding Patan also offer serene settings for yoga and meditation retreats, allowing you to connect with nature and find tranquility amidst the majestic Himalayas.

For the art and culture enthusiasts, Patan Durbar Square is a treasure trove of traditional arts and crafts. Immerse yourself in the world of thangka painting and woodcarving, as you witness skilled artisans creating masterpieces that have been passed down through generations. You can even try your hand at these ancient crafts and take home a piece of Nepal's cultural heritage.

The city of Patan also offers unique experiences for those seeking an authentic taste of Nepal's rural life. Homestays and community-based tourism initiatives allow you to live with local families, experience their way of life, and contribute to their sustainable development. You can also explore tea plantations and organic farms, learning about traditional farming practices and enjoying the fresh produce straight from the land.

As you leave Patan Durbar Square, don't forget to embark on a mountaineering or climbing expedition in the Himalayas. Nepal is renowned for its challenging peaks, and the city of Patan serves as a gateway to these majestic mountains. Whether you are a seasoned mountaineer or a novice climber, the Himalayas offer a once-in-a-lifetime adventure that will leave you in awe of nature's grandeur.

In conclusion, Patan Durbar Square is a melting pot of cultural heritage, adventure, spirituality, and natural beauty. Whether you are a trekking enthusiast, an art lover, a wildlife enthusiast, or someone seeking a spiritual retreat, Patan Durbar Square has something to offer everyone. So, pack your bags, embark on this incredible journey, and let Patan Durbar Square leave an indelible mark on your soul.

Lumbini - Birthplace of Lord Buddha

Welcome to the enchanting town of Lumbini, nestled in the plains of Nepal. This sacred place holds immense significance as it is the birthplace of Lord Buddha, the founder of Buddhism. As you embark on your journey to the rooftop of the world, a visit to Lumbini is an absolute must.

Lumbini is a serene and peaceful destination that attracts tourists from all corners of the globe. For those interested in trekking in the Himalayas, Lumbini serves as the perfect starting point. The town is surrounded by lush green landscapes and offers breathtaking views of the snow-capped peaks of the Himalayas. It is a haven for nature enthusiasts who can explore the nearby national parks and indulge in wildlife and birdwatching.

For the spiritually inclined, Lumbini is a haven for Buddhist monasteries and spiritual retreats. The ambiance is calm and tranquil, allowing visitors to immerse themselves in meditation and self-reflection. The ancient monasteries offer a glimpse into the teachings of Lord Buddha and provide a sacred space for those seeking spiritual enlightenment.

Adventure seekers will find their thrill in Lumbini as well. The town offers a range of adventure sports such as paragliding, rafting, and bungee jumping. Imagine the adrenaline rush as you soar through the skies or conquer the raging rapids of the rivers. Lumbini is the perfect destination for those seeking an adrenaline-fueled adventure.

If yoga and meditation are more to your liking, Lumbini provides the ideal setting for yoga and meditation retreats. Surrounded by the majestic Himalayas, you can practice yoga and meditation in the lap of nature, rejuvenating your mind, body, and soul. The serene atmosphere and tranquil surroundings make Lumbini an ideal retreat for those seeking inner peace and harmony.

Lumbini is not only a place of spirituality and adventure but also a treasure trove of cultural heritage. The town is home to ancient cities and cultural heritage sites that provide a glimpse into the rich history and traditions of Nepal. Explore the ancient cities, marvel at the intricate thangka paintings and wood carvings, and immerse yourself in the traditional arts and crafts of Nepal.

For those interested in sustainable tourism, Lumbini offers homestays and community-based tourism experiences in rural Nepal. Experience the warmth and hospitality of the locals as you stay in traditional homes and engage in organic farming experiences. This unique form of tourism allows you to connect with the local community and contribute to their livelihood.

Lumbini is a gateway to the majestic Himalayas, offering mountaineering and climbing expeditions for the adventurous souls. Conquer the towering peaks and challenge yourself as you embark on a mountaineering expedition of a lifetime.

In conclusion, Lumbini is a destination that caters to a diverse range of interests. Whether you seek spirituality, adventure, cultural immersion, or a connection with nature, Lumbini has something for everyone. Discover the birthplace of Lord Buddha and embark on a journey that will leave you with memories to last a lifetime.

Chapter 8: Tea Plantation Tours and Organic Farming Experiences

Discovering the tea culture of Nepal

Nestled in the lap of the mighty Himalayas, Nepal is not only a paradise for trekkers and adventure enthusiasts but also a haven for tea lovers. The tea culture of Nepal is as rich and diverse as its breathtaking landscapes, and exploring it is an experience that should not be missed.

Tea plantations in Nepal are mainly located in the eastern hilly regions, where the climate and altitude are perfect for growing high-quality tea. The lush green tea gardens, spread across terraced slopes, offer a picturesque view that is bound to captivate any nature lover. As you embark on a tea plantation tour, you will have the opportunity to witness the entire tea-making process, from plucking the leaves to processing and packaging.

Nepal is renowned for its organic tea, which is grown without the use of any synthetic fertilizers or pesticides. The tea farmers here take great pride in producing tea that is not only delicious but also environmentally sustainable. During your visit, you can learn about the traditional methods of organic farming and gain a deeper understanding of the importance of sustainable agriculture.

Tea tasting sessions are a highlight of any tea plantation tour in Nepal. You will have the chance to savor a variety of teas, each with its unique flavor and aroma. From delicate white teas to robust black teas, Nepal offers a wide range of options to satisfy every tea connoisseur's palate.

For those seeking a holistic experience, Nepal's tea gardens also provide a serene setting for yoga and meditation retreats. Imagine practicing your asanas amidst the tranquility of the tea fields, surrounded by the majestic

Himalayan peaks. This combination of natural beauty and spiritual rejuvenation is truly unparalleled.

Apart from the tea gardens, Nepal is also home to several tea houses and cafes, where you can immerse yourself in the local tea culture. Indulge in a cup of steaming chai or try the famous butter tea, a traditional Tibetan beverage. These cozy establishments not only serve delicious teas but also offer a glimpse into the daily lives of the local people.

In conclusion, exploring the tea culture of Nepal is a must for any tourist visiting this enchanting country. Whether you are a tea enthusiast, a nature lover, or a seeker of spiritual solace, Nepal's tea gardens have something to offer everyone. So, take a sip of Nepal's rich heritage and let the flavors of its tea transport you to a world of serenity and bliss.

Tea plantation tours in Ilam and Dhankuta

Nepal is not only known for its breathtaking mountain ranges but also for its rich cultural heritage and diverse landscapes. Among these landscapes, the tea plantations in Ilam and Dhankuta offer a unique and immersive experience for tourists seeking a taste of Nepal's agricultural traditions.

Ilam, located in the eastern part of Nepal, is famous for its tea gardens that stretch as far as the eye can see. The lush green tea plantations, set against the backdrop of majestic mountains, create a serene and picturesque environment. Visitors can embark on guided tours through the tea gardens, where they can witness the entire tea production process - from plucking the leaves to processing and packaging. They can even try their hand at plucking tea leaves, under the guidance of experienced plantation workers.

Dhankuta, another region renowned for its tea production, offers an equally captivating experience. The tea estates in this area provide an opportunity for tourists to learn about organic farming practices and sustainable agriculture. Visitors can explore the tea gardens, learn about the different varieties of tea, and savor a cup of freshly brewed tea in the midst of the plantations. The tours also allow visitors to interact with local farmers and gain insights into their daily lives and cultural practices.

For tea enthusiasts, these tours offer a chance to deepen their knowledge and appreciation for tea. They can learn about the intricacies of tea cultivation, the various types of tea, and the art of tea tasting. Additionally, visitors can purchase high-quality tea directly from the estates, ensuring the freshest and most authentic flavors.

Tea plantation tours in Ilam and Dhankuta are not only about tea; they also provide an opportunity to immerse oneself in the natural beauty of the surroundings. The tea gardens are often located in close proximity to national parks, offering opportunities for wildlife and birdwatching. Tourists can spot rare bird species, such as the Himalayan Monal and Rufous-necked Hornbill, as well as other wildlife like deer, langurs, and even leopards.

In conclusion, tea plantation tours in Ilam and Dhankuta offer a delightful blend of cultural immersion, natural beauty, and agricultural experiences. Whether you are a tea lover, a nature enthusiast, or simply seeking a unique adventure, these tours provide an unforgettable journey into the heart of Nepal's tea culture.

Experiencing organic farming in rural Nepal

As you embark on your journey to the rooftop of the world, there is an extraordinary opportunity that awaits you in the rural corners of Nepal - the chance to immerse yourself in the world of organic farming. Nestled amidst the breathtaking Himalayan landscapes, this subchapter will take you on a captivating exploration of the sustainable agricultural practices that have been passed down through generations in this remote region.

Venturing off the beaten path, you will discover the hidden gems of rural Nepal, where lush green fields stretch as far as the eye can see. Here, in the heart of nature, farmers have embraced the principles of organic farming, cultivating their land without the use of synthetic chemicals or genetically modified organisms. This sustainable approach not only preserves the natural environment but also ensures the production of healthy and nutritious crops.

During your visit, you will have the opportunity to work alongside these dedicated farmers, getting your hands dirty as you learn about their traditional farming techniques. From sowing seeds to tending to the fields, you will experience the joys and challenges of a farmer's life firsthand. Embrace the simplicity of daily routines and gain a deeper understanding of the intricate relationship between humans and the land they cultivate.

As you engage in this unique cultural exchange, you will witness the interconnectedness of the local community and their harmonious coexistence with nature. Share stories and laughter with your hosts as you indulge in traditional meals made from the bountiful produce of the farm. Through this authentic experience, you will gain a profound appreciation for the sustainable practices that lie at the heart of rural Nepali life.

Moreover, this encounter with organic farming will leave a lasting impact on your own understanding of sustainable living. Take the lessons learned in Nepal back home and incorporate them into your daily life, becoming an advocate for organic farming in your own community.

So, whether you are a nature enthusiast, a sustainable living advocate, or simply seeking a unique cultural experience, don't miss the opportunity to engage in organic farming in rural Nepal. Discover the beauty of sustainable agriculture, connect with the land, and leave with a renewed sense of appreciation for the delicate balance between humans and nature.

Chapter 9: Mountaineering and Climbing Expeditions in the Himalayas

Conquering the highest peaks in the world

Welcome to the subchapter on "Conquering the highest peaks in the world" from our book, "Journey to the Rooftop of the World: Trekking in the Himalayas". For all the adventure enthusiasts out there, this section is tailored just for you.

The Himalayas, with its majestic peaks, have always been a magnet for mountaineers from around the globe. Nepal, being home to eight of the fourteen highest peaks in the world, including Mount Everest, offers an unparalleled experience for mountaineering and climbing expeditions.

Embarking on a mountaineering expedition in the Himalayas is not for the faint-hearted. It requires physical endurance, mental strength, and a passion for adventure. But the rewards are beyond measure. Standing on the summit of a Himalayan peak, gazing at the breathtaking vistas, is an experience that will stay with you forever.

However, conquering these giants requires careful planning and preparation. It is essential to hire experienced guides and sherpas who can navigate the treacherous terrain and ensure your safety. They will also provide you with valuable insights into the local culture and traditions, making your journey not just about the climb but also about the people and their way of life.

While mountaineering is the main highlight, Nepal offers a plethora of other activities for adventure enthusiasts. From paragliding over the stunning landscapes, rafting in the gushing rivers, to bungee jumping from towering suspension bridges, Nepal is a playground for adrenaline junkies.

For those seeking a more serene experience, the Himalayas also offer yoga and meditation retreats in the mountains. Immerse yourself in the tranquil surroundings, learn from experienced gurus, and find inner peace amidst nature's beauty.

Nepal is not just about adventure; it is also a treasure trove of cultural heritage. Explore ancient cities and UNESCO World Heritage Sites, immerse yourself in the vibrant traditions of thangka painting and wood carving, or embark on a journey to Buddhist monasteries and spiritual retreats to discover the spiritual side of Nepal.

For wildlife enthusiasts, Nepal's national parks are a paradise. Witness the majestic Bengal tigers, rare one-horned rhinoceros, and a myriad of bird species in their natural habitat. Get up close and personal with nature at its finest.

To have a truly immersive experience, consider staying in homestays and participating in community-based tourism in rural Nepal. Engage with locals, learn about their customs, and contribute to their sustainable development.

So, whether you are an adventure seeker, a spiritual explorer, a nature lover, or a cultural enthusiast, Nepal has something to offer for everyone. Come, embark on this extraordinary journey to conquer the highest peaks in the world and discover the many wonders of the Himalayas.

Climbing Mount Everest

Embarking on a journey to climb Mount Everest is a once-in-a-lifetime experience that pushes the boundaries of human endurance. As the highest peak in the world, reaching its summit at 8,848 meters is an achievement that only a brave and determined few can claim. In this subchapter, we will delve into the challenges, triumphs, and rewards of climbing this majestic mountain.

Before setting foot on Everest, it is crucial to be well-prepared physically and mentally. Training and acclimatization are essential to overcome the harsh conditions and extreme altitudes. Hiring an experienced guide and joining a reputable expedition team is highly recommended to ensure safety and success. These experts will guide you through the treacherous terrain, help you navigate the ever-changing weather conditions, and provide valuable support every step of the way.

The journey to Everest Base Camp, the starting point for most climbers, is an adventure in itself. Trekking through breathtaking valleys, picturesque Sherpa villages, and ancient Buddhist monasteries, you will immerse yourself in the rich culture and traditions of the Himalayas. Along the way, keep an eye out for rare wildlife and colorful bird species found in the national parks, making for an unforgettable wildlife and birdwatching experience.

For adventure enthusiasts, Nepal offers a myriad of adrenaline-pumping activities. Paragliding over the stunning landscapes, rafting down raging rivers, and bungee jumping off towering cliffs are just a few of the heart-pounding options available. After such intense activities, find solace in the tranquility of the mountains by joining a yoga and meditation retreat, where you can rejuvenate your mind, body, and soul.

Nepal is also a treasure trove of cultural heritage sites and ancient cities. Explore the UNESCO World Heritage Sites, such as the mystical Kathmandu Durbar Square and the serene Bhaktapur, where traditional arts and crafts like thangka painting and wood carving thrive. Take a break from the mountains and visit tea plantations, immersing yourself in the soothing aroma of freshly brewed tea and learning about organic farming practices.

For those seeking the ultimate adventure, mountaineering and climbing expeditions in the Himalayas provide the perfect challenge. Whether you choose to conquer the mighty Everest or opt for other peaks, the sense of accomplishment and awe-inspiring views will leave an indelible mark on your soul.

Lastly, for a truly authentic experience, consider staying in a homestay and engaging in community-based tourism in rural Nepal. Connect with the locals, learn about their traditions, and contribute to the sustainable development of these remote areas.

Climbing Mount Everest is not just an adventure; it is a transformative journey that will test your physical limits, expand your cultural horizons, and ignite your spirit of exploration. So, lace up your boots, pack your determination, and prepare for an experience unlike any other on the rooftop of the world.

Annapurna Mountain Range expeditions

The Annapurna Mountain Range in Nepal is a dream destination for adventure enthusiasts from all around the world. Offering a wide range of experiences, from trekking to mountaineering, this subchapter will guide you through the breathtaking wonders of the Annapurna region.

Trekking in the Annapurna Range is a popular activity that attracts thousands of tourists each year. With a variety of treks available, ranging from easy to challenging, there is something for everyone. The Annapurna Circuit Trek is one of the most famous, taking you on a journey around the entire range, offering stunning views of snow-capped peaks, lush valleys, and traditional villages.

For those seeking a spiritual retreat, the Annapurna region is home to several Buddhist monasteries and meditation centers. Immerse yourself in the tranquil atmosphere, learn from experienced monks, and discover the ancient teachings of Buddhism. The peaceful surroundings and majestic mountains will create the perfect environment for self-reflection and rejuvenation.

Wildlife and birdwatching enthusiasts will also find their paradise in the Annapurna region. The Annapurna Conservation Area is home to a diverse range of species, including elusive snow leopards, Himalayan tahr, and numerous bird species. Embark on a safari-style trek and witness these incredible creatures in their natural habitat.

Adventure sports enthusiasts can also find their adrenaline fix in the Annapurna region. From paragliding over the picturesque Pokhara Valley to white-water rafting down the roaring rivers, there are plenty of thrilling activities to choose from. If you're feeling particularly adventurous, why not try bungee jumping from one of the highest suspension bridges in Nepal?

For those seeking a more serene experience, the Annapurna region also offers yoga and meditation retreats amidst the majestic mountains. Disconnect from the hustle and bustle of everyday life and find inner peace in the tranquil surroundings. Experienced instructors will guide you through various practices, helping you achieve a state of mindfulness and relaxation.

In addition to the natural wonders, the Annapurna region is also rich in cultural heritage sites and ancient cities. Explore the historic city of Pokhara, visit the UNESCO World Heritage Site of Bhaktapur, or marvel at the ancient temples of Kathmandu. Each step will take you deeper into the rich cultural tapestry of Nepal.

Tea plantation tours and organic farming experiences are also gaining popularity in the Annapurna region. Learn about sustainable farming practices, pick your own tea leaves, and indulge in the flavors of freshly brewed organic tea. Immerse yourself in the local way of life and gain a deeper understanding of the importance of sustainable agriculture.

Mountaineering and climbing expeditions are another highlight of the Annapurna region. With several peaks above 7,000 meters, including the iconic Annapurna I, climbers from around the globe flock to test their skills and conquer these majestic summits. Experienced guides and support teams ensure a safe and exhilarating experience.

For those interested in traditional arts and crafts, the Annapurna region offers opportunities to learn thangka painting and wood carving. Immerse yourself in the rich artistic heritage of Nepal and try your hand at these ancient crafts. Local artisans will guide you through the process, allowing you to create your own unique masterpiece.

To truly experience the warmth and hospitality of the Nepali people, consider staying in a homestay or participating in community-based tourism in rural Nepal. Live with a local family, learn about their customs and traditions, and contribute to sustainable development in remote communities. This immersive experience will leave a lasting impact on your journey.

The Annapurna Mountain Range expeditions offer a diverse range of experiences that cater to the interests of every traveler. Whether you seek adventure, spiritual enlightenment, or cultural immersion, this region has it all. Embark on a journey to the rooftop of the world and create memories that will last a lifetime.

Training and equipment required for mountaineering

Mountaineering in the Himalayas is an exhilarating adventure that requires proper training and equipment to ensure a safe and successful expedition. Whether you are a seasoned climber or a first-time adventurer, it is essential to be well-prepared for the challenges that lie ahead. In this subchapter, we will discuss the training and equipment required for mountaineering in the Himalayas.

Training is crucial before embarking on a mountaineering expedition. It is highly recommended to undergo physical training to build stamina, strength, and endurance. Regular cardio exercises such as running, hiking, and cycling can improve your cardiovascular fitness. Strength training exercises like weightlifting and resistance training can help develop the muscles needed for climbing. Additionally, practicing yoga can enhance flexibility and balance, which are vital for mountaineering.

Furthermore, it is essential to acquire technical skills specific to mountaineering. These skills include rope handling, ice climbing, crevasse rescue, and navigation. Participating in mountaineering courses or hiring experienced guides can help you gain these skills and provide valuable knowledge about the mountains, weather patterns, and emergency procedures.

Besides training, having the right equipment is crucial for a safe and successful mountaineering expedition. Here are some essential items:

1. Climbing gear: This includes crampons, ice axes, harnesses, helmets, and ropes. These tools are essential for navigating icy slopes and crevasses.

2. Clothing: Layering is key to staying warm in the harsh mountain environment. It is recommended to have waterproof and windproof outer layers, insulating mid-layers, and moisture-wicking base layers. Don't forget warm hats, gloves, and socks.

3. Footwear: Mountaineering boots with crampon compatibility are necessary for tackling steep and icy terrain. Make sure they are comfortable and provide sufficient ankle support.

4. Camping gear: A sturdy tent, sleeping bag, sleeping pad, and cooking equipment are essential for overnight stays in high-altitude camps.

5. Safety equipment: Carry a first aid kit, emergency shelter, headlamp, and communication device for any unforeseen circumstances.

Remember, mountaineering is a physically demanding and risky activity. It is crucial to ensure that you have proper training, experience, and equipment before attempting any climb in the Himalayas. Always prioritize safety and adhere to the guidance of experienced guides or mountaineering experts. With the right preparation, you can embark on an unforgettable and rewarding mountaineering experience in the Himalayas.

Chapter 10: Traditional Arts and Crafts of Nepal

Thangka painting - a window to spirituality

In the vast realm of Nepalese art, Thangka painting stands as a window to spirituality. This ancient form of religious art offers a glimpse into the rich cultural heritage and profound spirituality that permeates the Himalayan region. For tourists embarking on a journey to the rooftop of the world, understanding Thangka painting is essential to truly appreciating the depth of the Himalayan experience.

Thangka paintings are not mere works of art; they are sacred objects that hold immense spiritual significance. Intricately painted on cotton or silk, Thangkas depict deities, mandalas, and other divine subjects, serving as visual aids for meditation and spiritual practice. Each stroke of the brush, each vivid color, and each delicate detail is crafted with utmost precision, imbuing the Thangka with a divine presence.

To delve deeper into the world of Thangka painting, a visit to the Buddhist monasteries and spiritual retreats of Nepal is a must. Here, one can witness the art form in its natural habitat, with monks and artisans meticulously working on Thangkas. The monasteries offer a serene environment, allowing visitors to witness the meditative process behind these intricate masterpieces. Engaging in conversations with the monks and artists provides invaluable insights into the symbolism and spiritual significance of each painting.

For those seeking a more adventurous experience, wildlife and birdwatching in national parks offer an opportunity to witness the natural beauty that inspires Thangka artists. The breathtaking landscapes and diverse fauna of Nepal provide inspiration for the vibrant colors and intricate depictions found in Thangka paintings.

Moreover, Nepal's cultural heritage sites and ancient cities offer a treasure trove of Thangka art. From the bustling streets of Kathmandu's Thamel district to the serene courtyards of Bhaktapur, travelers can explore numerous galleries and workshops that showcase the work of skilled Thangka artists. Many of these artists offer workshops and classes, allowing visitors to try their hand at this ancient art form under the guidance of experts.

In conclusion, Thangka painting is a gateway to spirituality, allowing tourists to immerse themselves in the rich cultural heritage and profound spirituality of the Himalayas. Whether through visits to Buddhist monasteries, engaging with local artists, or exploring the vibrant art scene of Nepal, delving into the world of Thangka painting is an essential part of any Himalayan adventure. So, open the window to spirituality and let Thangka paintings guide your journey to the rooftop of the world.

Wood carving - preserving ancient craftsmanship

Wood carving is an ancient craftsmanship that has been preserved and cherished for centuries in Nepal. This subchapter explores the rich tradition of wood carving in the Himalayas, providing insights into the techniques, significance, and cultural impact of this art form.

Nestled amidst the breathtaking landscapes of the Himalayas, Nepal is a treasure trove of ancient art forms. Wood carving, in particular, holds a special place in the hearts of the Nepalese people. Passed down through generations, this traditional craft has not only survived the test of time but has also evolved, adapting to changing tastes and preferences.

Wood carving in Nepal is an intricate process that requires immense skill and patience. Artisans meticulously hand-carve wood to create stunning sculptures, intricate furniture, and decorative items. The mastery lies in the ability to transform a simple piece of wood into a work of art, with each stroke of the chisel bringing life and character to the wood.

The significance of wood carving goes beyond its aesthetic appeal. Many of the carvings depict religious and spiritual motifs, reflecting the deep-rooted traditions and beliefs of the Nepalese people. Buddhist monasteries are adorned with intricately carved wooden pillars, windows, and doors, giving them a distinct architectural charm. These carvings not only enhance the visual appeal of the monasteries but also serve as a medium for transmitting religious teachings and stories.

Tourists visiting Nepal can witness the mesmerizing craftsmanship of wood carving by exploring the ancient cities and cultural heritage sites. The cities of Kathmandu, Bhaktapur, and Patan are renowned for their ornate wooden architecture, showcasing the exceptional skills of Nepalese wood carvers. Visitors can also visit wood carving workshops and interact with the artisans to gain a deeper understanding of this ancient craft.

For those seeking a more immersive experience, homestays and community-based tourism in rural Nepal provide an opportunity to witness wood carving in its authentic setting. These experiences offer a glimpse into the daily lives of the artisans, allowing tourists to appreciate their dedication and passion for their craft.

Wood carving is not just an art form; it is a reflection of Nepal's rich cultural heritage. By supporting and promoting this ancient craftsmanship, tourists can contribute to the preservation of Nepal's traditional arts and crafts. Whether you are a trekking enthusiast, a spiritual seeker, or an adventure lover, exploring the world of wood carving in Nepal will undoubtedly enrich your journey to the rooftop of the world.

Exploring traditional handicrafts in Kathmandu

Kathmandu, the capital city of Nepal, is a treasure trove of traditional handicrafts that reflect the rich cultural heritage of the country. For tourists with an interest in traditional arts and crafts, Kathmandu offers a unique opportunity to witness the skills and techniques passed down through generations.

One of the most prominent traditional handicrafts in Kathmandu is thangka painting. These intricate paintings are created on cotton or silk fabric and depict various Buddhist deities and scenes. The process involves meticulous brushwork and intricate detailing, resulting in breathtakingly beautiful artworks. Visitors can watch thangka painters at work and even try their hand at creating their own masterpiece under the guidance of skilled artisans.

Wood carving is another traditional craft that flourishes in Kathmandu. Skilled artisans create intricate designs on wooden doors, windows, and furniture using traditional tools. The level of craftsmanship is awe-inspiring, and visitors can witness the process up close in the bustling markets and workshops of the city. From intricately carved doors of ancient temples to delicate wooden figurines, the art of wood carving in Kathmandu is a testament to the skill and dedication of Nepali artisans.

For those interested in learning more about traditional handicrafts, Kathmandu offers numerous workshops and classes where visitors can learn the basics of thangka painting or wood carving. These hands-on experiences provide a deeper understanding of the techniques and cultural significance behind these crafts.

In addition to thangka painting and wood carving, Kathmandu is also known for its vibrant markets where visitors can find an array of traditional handicrafts. From colorful textiles and pottery to handwoven rugs and jewelry, the markets of Kathmandu offer a kaleidoscope of traditional crafts that make for unique souvenirs.

Exploring the traditional handicrafts of Kathmandu is not only a way to appreciate the artistic skills of the Nepali people but also a means to support local artisans and preserve the cultural heritage of the region. Whether it's watching artists at work, trying your hand at traditional crafts, or simply browsing through the bustling markets, the traditional arts and crafts of Kathmandu are sure to leave a lasting impression on any visitor.

Chapter 11: Homestays and Community-Based Tourism in Rural Nepal

Immersing in local culture through homestays

One of the most enriching experiences while trekking in the Himalayas is the opportunity to immerse oneself in the local culture through homestays. Far beyond the typical tourist experience, homestays offer a unique chance to truly connect with the people, traditions, and way of life in rural Nepal.

Homestays provide an authentic glimpse into the daily lives of the local communities. Visitors have the chance to live with a local family, sharing meals, stories, and laughter. This intimate setting allows tourists to forge genuine connections, gaining a deeper understanding of the local customs and traditions that have shaped the region for centuries.

During a homestay, guests can participate in various activities alongside their hosts. This might include helping with household chores, working in the fields, or learning traditional crafts such as thangka painting or wood carving. By actively engaging in these activities, tourists not only gain new skills but also contribute to the sustainable development of the community.

The benefits of homestays extend beyond cultural immersion. By choosing community-based tourism, visitors directly support the local economy, ensuring that the profits stay within the community. This becomes particularly important for rural areas, where economic opportunities are limited. Homestays empower local people, providing them with a sustainable source of income while preserving their cultural heritage.

Moreover, staying in a village homestay allows tourists to witness the stunning natural beauty that surrounds these communities. Waking up to panoramic views of the Himalayan peaks or exploring the nearby national parks for wildlife and birdwatching are experiences that cannot be replicated in any other setting. Adventure enthusiasts can also indulge in thrilling activities such as paragliding, rafting, and bungee jumping, adding an extra dash of excitement to their stay.

For those seeking a more spiritual experience, homestays near Buddhist monasteries and spiritual retreats provide the perfect opportunity for meditation and self-reflection. The peaceful atmosphere and serene surroundings of the mountains offer a tranquil escape from the chaos of everyday life, allowing visitors to reconnect with their inner selves.

In conclusion, immersing in local culture through homestays is an invaluable experience for tourists trekking in the Himalayas. The opportunity to live with local families, engage in traditional activities, and support the community offers a truly authentic and sustainable travel experience. Whether one is interested in adventure sports, spiritual retreats, or cultural heritage, homestays provide a gateway to the diverse wonders of rural Nepal.

Supporting sustainable tourism initiatives

As tourists, it is essential for us to be mindful of the impact our travels have on the destinations we visit. The Himalayas, with its breathtaking landscapes and diverse cultural heritage, is a region that heavily relies on tourism. To ensure the preservation of its natural beauty and cultural richness, it is crucial for us to support sustainable tourism initiatives.

Trekking in the Himalayas is a popular activity that attracts thousands of adventurers each year. When planning your trek, choose a tour operator or guide who follows sustainable practices. Look for companies that prioritize responsible waste management, promote eco-friendly accommodations, and support local communities. By doing so, you are contributing to the conservation of the fragile Himalayan ecosystem and ensuring that future generations can also enjoy this incredible experience.

Buddhist monasteries and spiritual retreats are another highlight of the Himalayan region. When visiting these sacred sites, show respect for the local customs and traditions. Seek opportunities to learn about Buddhism and engage in meaningful cultural exchanges with the monks and nuns. Many monasteries also offer meditation retreats, which not only provide a spiritual experience but also support the local economy.

Wildlife and birdwatching in national parks is a must-do for nature enthusiasts. However, it is essential to observe these animals and birds from a safe distance and avoid disturbing their natural habitats. Support national parks and conservation organizations that work to protect the fragile ecosystems and endangered species in the region.

For adventure enthusiasts, Nepal offers a range of thrilling activities such as paragliding, rafting, and bungee jumping. When participating in these activities, choose operators who prioritize safety and adhere to responsible tourism practices. Ensure that the equipment used is of good quality and regularly maintained. By supporting responsible adventure sports operators, you are contributing to the safety of both yourself and the environment.

Yoga and meditation retreats in the mountains provide an opportunity for relaxation and self-discovery. Choose retreats that promote sustainability, use eco-friendly practices, and support local communities. By practicing yoga and meditation in harmony with nature, you are not only benefiting yourself but also supporting the preservation of the Himalayan environment.

Cultural heritage sites and ancient cities of Nepal offer a glimpse into its rich history and traditions. When visiting these sites, respect the local customs, and follow the guidelines set by heritage conservation organizations. Many of these sites have sustainable tourism initiatives in place, including waste management and preservation efforts. By supporting these initiatives, you are helping to protect Nepal's cultural heritage for future generations.

Tea plantation tours and organic farming experiences provide a unique opportunity to learn about sustainable agricultural practices. Choose tours that promote organic farming methods and support local farmers. By purchasing locally produced tea and organic products, you are contributing to the livelihoods of rural communities and supporting sustainable agriculture.

Mountaineering and climbing expeditions in the Himalayas are physically demanding activities that require careful planning and preparation. Choose operators who prioritize safety, follow ethical guidelines, and promote responsible climbing practices. By supporting responsible mountaineering operators, you are ensuring the safety of climbers and minimizing the impact on the fragile Himalayan ecosystem.

Traditional arts and crafts of Nepal, such as thangka painting and wood carving, are an integral part of its cultural heritage. When purchasing souvenirs, choose authentic handicrafts made by local artisans. By supporting traditional arts and crafts, you are contributing to the preservation of these traditional skills and supporting local livelihoods.

Homestays and community-based tourism in rural Nepal offer a unique opportunity to experience the local way of life and support rural communities. Choose homestays that are part of community-based tourism initiatives, which aim to empower local communities and preserve their cultural heritage. By staying in a homestay, you are directly supporting the local economy and gaining a deeper understanding of the local culture.

In conclusion, supporting sustainable tourism initiatives is crucial for the preservation of the Himalayas' natural beauty, cultural heritage, and the well-being of local communities. By making conscious choices as tourists, we can ensure that the Himalayas remain a pristine and vibrant destination for generations to come.

Experiencing traditional Nepali hospitality in rural communities

Nepal, with its breathtaking landscapes and diverse culture, has long been a popular destination for adventurous travelers. While the country is renowned for its towering peaks and challenging treks, there is another aspect of Nepal that often goes unnoticed – its warm and welcoming rural communities. In this subchapter, we will explore the unique opportunity to experience traditional Nepali hospitality in these rural communities.

As you venture off the beaten path, you will find yourself immersed in the daily lives of the locals, who are known for their genuine warmth and generosity. The people of rural Nepal open their homes and hearts to visitors, offering a rare glimpse into their traditions and way of life. Homestays in these communities provide an authentic and enriching experience, allowing you to forge deep connections and learn about the local culture firsthand.

During your stay, you will have the chance to participate in various activities that showcase the rich heritage of Nepal. From traditional dance performances to hands-on workshops in traditional arts and crafts such as thangka painting and wood carving, you will gain a deeper appreciation for the skill and artistry of the Nepali people.

One of the highlights of your visit will undoubtedly be the local cuisine. Nepali food is a delicious blend of flavors, influenced by neighboring countries like India and Tibet. You will have the opportunity to savor traditional dishes prepared with locally sourced ingredients, giving you a true taste of Nepal.

Beyond the cultural experiences, community-based tourism in rural Nepal also offers you the chance to contribute to the well-being of these communities. By staying in a homestay or supporting local initiatives, you will directly contribute to the livelihoods of the people, helping to preserve their way of life for future generations.

Whether you choose to embark on a trek through the picturesque villages of the Annapurna region or opt for a more off-the-beaten-path experience in remote corners of the country, experiencing traditional Nepali hospitality in rural communities will undoubtedly be a highlight of your journey. The warmth and kindness of the locals, combined with the stunning natural beauty of Nepal, will leave a lasting impression on your heart and soul.

So, pack your bags and get ready to embark on a journey that goes beyond the mountains – a journey that takes you deep into the heart of Nepal's rural communities, where traditional hospitality and cultural immersion await you.

Chapter 12: Conclusion

Reflecting on the transformative journey in the Himalayas

The majestic Himalayas have long been a magnet for adventurers, spiritual seekers, and nature enthusiasts alike. Journeying to the rooftop of the world is a transformative experience that leaves an indelible mark on the souls of those who dare to venture into its awe-inspiring landscapes. In this subchapter, we invite you to reflect on the profound journey you have embarked upon in the Himalayas and how it has the power to change you.

Trekking in the Himalayas is a popular activity that allows you to immerse yourself in the breathtaking beauty of the mountains. As you traverse rugged trails, surrounded by snow-capped peaks and pristine valleys, you will discover the strength within yourself and the resilience needed to conquer any obstacle. The Himalayas have a way of pushing you past your limits, challenging your body, mind, and spirit, and ultimately transforming you into a stronger, more determined individual.

Buddhist monasteries and spiritual retreats are sanctuaries of tranquility nestled amidst the Himalayan peaks. Here, you can delve deep into the teachings of Buddhism, practice meditation, and find inner peace. The serene and serene environment of these monasteries allows for reflection and introspection, enabling you to connect with your inner self and gain a deeper understanding of life's purpose.

For wildlife enthusiasts and birdwatchers, the national parks of the Himalayas offer a treasure trove of biodiversity. From the elusive snow leopard to the colorful Himalayan Monal, these parks are a haven for nature lovers. As you witness the wonders of the animal kingdom in their natural habitat, you will be reminded of the interconnectedness of all living beings and the importance of preserving our fragile ecosystem.

Adventure sports in Nepal bring an adrenaline rush like no other. Whether you're paragliding over the valleys, rafting down the raging rivers, or bungee jumping from towering suspension bridges, these thrilling activities will push you out of your comfort zone and leave you with unforgettable memories.

Yoga and meditation retreats in the mountains offer a chance to rejuvenate your body, mind, and soul. Surrounded by the serene beauty of nature, you can practice yoga asanas, learn ancient breathing techniques, and cultivate mindfulness. The Himalayas provide the perfect backdrop for self-discovery and inner transformation.

Nepal's cultural heritage sites and ancient cities are a testament to the rich history and vibrant traditions of this land. Exploring ancient temples, royal palaces, and UNESCO World Heritage sites will transport you back in time and allow you to appreciate the cultural diversity of Nepal.

Tea plantation tours and organic farming experiences offer a glimpse into the sustainable practices that have been passed down through generations. You can witness the meticulous process of tea cultivation or participate in organic farming, connecting with the earth and gaining a deeper appreciation for the importance of sustainable living.

Mountaineering and climbing expeditions in the Himalayas are the ultimate test of physical and mental endurance. Scaling the towering peaks requires determination, discipline, and teamwork. The Himalayas will teach you the value of perseverance and the rewards of pushing beyond your limits.

Traditional arts and crafts of Nepal, such as thangka painting and wood carving, showcase the artistic prowess of the Nepali people. By engaging in these crafts, you can tap into your creative side and learn about the cultural significance behind these ancient art forms.

Homestays and community-based tourism in rural Nepal offer an opportunity to immerse yourself in the local way of life. By staying with local families, you can experience their warm hospitality, learn about their customs and traditions, and contribute to the sustainable development of rural communities.

In conclusion, embarking on a transformative journey in the Himalayas is an experience that transcends the boundaries of time and space. Whether you're seeking adventure, spiritual enlightenment, or cultural immersion, the Himalayas have something to offer to every traveler. As you reflect on your journey, you will realize that the transformative power of the Himalayas lies not only in its majestic landscapes but also in the profound impact it has on your inner self.

Inspiring others to embark on their own adventure

Embarking on a journey to the Rooftop of the World is an experience that will leave you forever changed. The Himalayas, with its majestic peaks, serene landscapes, and rich cultural heritage, offer a multitude of activities and attractions that cater to every traveler's interests. From trekking through breathtaking trails to exploring ancient cities and monasteries, Nepal has something for everyone. In this subchapter, we aim to inspire our readers to embark on their own adventure and discover the wonders that await them in this enchanting country.

For those seeking a thrilling and physically challenging experience, trekking in the Himalayas is an absolute must. Traverse through spectacular landscapes, lush valleys, and remote villages while immersing yourself in the local culture. The mesmerizing views of snow-capped peaks and the warm hospitality of the locals will surely leave a lasting impression.

If spirituality is your calling, explore the Buddhist monasteries and spiritual retreats nestled amidst the mountains. Discover inner peace and tranquility as you meditate in these serene settings and learn from wise monks who have dedicated their lives to spiritual enlightenment.

Nature enthusiasts will be delighted by the wildlife and birdwatching opportunities in the national parks of Nepal. Immerse yourself in the natural beauty of Chitwan or Bardia National Park, where you can spot rare and exotic wildlife, including the elusive Bengal tiger and the one-horned rhinoceros.

For adrenaline junkies, Nepal offers an array of adventure sports. Soar through the skies while paragliding, conquer raging rivers through exhilarating white water rafting, or take a leap of faith with bungee jumping. Test your limits and create unforgettable memories.

The Himalayas are also a haven for yoga and meditation enthusiasts. Retreat to the mountains and rejuvenate your mind, body, and soul through yoga and meditation practices. Immerse yourself in the tranquil surroundings and find inner peace amidst the awe-inspiring beauty of nature.

Explore the rich cultural heritage and ancient cities of Nepal, where you can witness the architectural marvels of Kathmandu Durbar Square, the mystical atmosphere of Bhaktapur, and the spiritual aura of Pashupatinath Temple. Lose yourself in the vibrant tapestry of Nepalese culture.

For those seeking unique experiences, indulge in tea plantation tours and organic farming experiences. Learn about the intricacies of tea production and immerse yourself in the simplicity of rural life. Discover the joy of sustainable farming practices and connect with nature on a deeper level.

If you have a passion for mountaineering and climbing, Nepal is the ultimate playground. Join a climbing expedition and conquer the world's highest peaks, including Mount Everest. Push your limits, challenge yourself, and experience the indescribable thrill of standing on top of the world.

Lastly, explore the traditional arts and crafts of Nepal, such as thangka painting and wood carving. Witness the intricate craftsmanship and learn from skilled artisans who have preserved these ancient techniques for generations.

And when you're ready to truly immerse yourself in Nepalese culture, opt for homestays and community-based tourism in rural Nepal. Experience the warmth and hospitality of the locals, learn about their traditions, and contribute to the sustainable development of these communities.

In conclusion, Nepal offers a diverse range of experiences that cater to all interests and passions. Whether you seek adventure, spirituality, cultural enrichment, or simply a chance to connect with nature, Nepal has it all. Allow this subchapter to inspire you to embark on your own adventure and create memories that will last a lifetime.